KILIM RUGS

TRIBAL TALES IN WOOL

SUSAN GOMERSALL

PHOTOGRAPHY BY BRUCE M. WATERS

Schiffer Publishing Ltd

4880 Lower Valley Road, Atglen, PA 19310 USA

Copyright © 1999 by Susan Gomersall

Library of Congress Cataloging-in-Publication Data
Gomersall, Susan
  Kilim rugs: tribal tales in wool / Susan
Gomersall; photography by Bruce M. Waters with
Tina Skinner.
     p. cm.
  ISBN: 0-7643-1158-1 (pbk.)
  1. Kilims--Asia, Central. 2. Rugs, Nomadic--Asia,
Central. I. Title.
NK2875 .G66 2000
746.7'2--dc21
                              00-008117

Cover design by Bruce Waters
Book design by Blair Loughrey
Type set in Zurich/Korinna

ISBN: 0-7643-1158-1
Printed in China
1 2 3 4

Published by Schiffer Publishing Ltd.
4880 Lower Valley Road
Atglen, PA 19310
Phone: (610) 593-1777; Fax: (610) 593-2002
E-mail: Schifferbk@aol.com
Please visit our web site catalog at
WWW.SCHIFFERBOOKS.COM

We are always looking for people to write books on new
and related subjects. If you have an idea for a book,
please contact us at the above address.

This book may be purchased from the publisher.
Include $3.95 for shipping. Please try your bookstore first.
You may write for a free catalog.

In Europe, Schiffer books are distributed by
Bushwood Books
6 Marksbury Ave. Kew Gardens
Surrey TW9 4JF England
Phone: 44 (0)208-392-8585; Fax: 44 (0)208-392-9876
E-mail: Bushwd@aol.com
Free postage in the UK. Europe: air mail at cost.
Please try your bookstore first.

CONTENTS

ACKNOWLEDGMENTS

I would like to dedicate this book in memory of Jim Donnelly. He was my friend, mentor, and teacher.

It is really important to thank all the amazing carpet dealers I have met during my travels. Without them I would never have found the quality or the quantity of rugs that I have. I would also like to thank my American business partner, Richard Starna, who patiently stays home and keeps the business afloat while I go off to Central Asia and spend all the money.

Perhaps the most thanks should go to all my customers past and present who have kept me afloat by believing in me and purchasing my goods. Special thanks go those earliest customers who believed me when I told them that a kilim rug isn't supposed to have a pile. And a million thanks go to Azy Schecter and Marcus Leatherdale for the generous contribution of their Waterfront Studio in DUMBO, Down Under Manhattan Bridge Overpass.

I thank you all.

INTRODUCTION

For many years, friends and customers have asked me to write a book about kilims, not because I am an expert, or that my technical knowledge is extraordinary, but because of my great love and enthusiasm for kilims and the people who weave them. I never studied rugs or textile design at college. I learnt my trade by buying, selling, touching, and, in some cases, by smelling my way through thousands of rugs. In this book I want to share with you my knowledge about the people who made these rugs, their histories and their particular stories.

Most importantly, I want someone who is contemplating buying a rug to enjoy that experience. So many times I've been asked by friends who have traveled and bought rugs in local bazaars, did I get a good deal? In reply I have three questions. Do you like it? Was the price right for you? Did you have fun? If the answers are yes, then in my opinion you got a good deal. I know that buying a rug can be a traumatic experience, you feel overwhelmed, you lack knowledge, and the general perception of rug dealers is that we are often far from honest. This book, I hope, will answer some questions that you always wanted to ask, but felt too intimidated to do so. Each chapter tells one tribe's story; a little bit of their history, a little bit about their present day circumstances, and descriptions of the rugs they weave. Both antique and modern rugs can be found in each chapter, along with some indication of what these generally cost in a retail situation. If you're interested in knowing how many knots per square inch or how the yarns are dyed, this is not a book for you. If you want to share my great stories and look at over two hundred fantastic color photographs of rugs from Central Asia, this is the book for you.

About Kilims

Kilims are flat woven rugs. This means that these rugs are not the "soft on the toes rugs" that many of us grew up with. The actual word kilim is found in Iran (Gelim), Afghanistan (Kelim), and Georgia (Kylym) and refers to the distinctive styles of weaving used for centuries by the nomadic tribes of these areas. I will discuss in individual chapters the many different types of weaving techniques that are classified as kilims, but in layman's terms, a kilim is a rug without a pile.

In the nineteenth century, the rug trade between Europe and the Orient was prolific. Kilims, however, took secondhand status. Western buyers prefered their thicker, more luxuriant, hand-knotted cousins. The story goes that in the 1900s, carpet exporters used kilims as wrapping material for their Oriental rugs. It is lucky for us that this was the fashion, as kilims did not suffer the fate of pile carpets, whose colors and designs were altered and manipulated to keep pace with current trends. This is why, even today, we find kilims being produced with designs and motifs that can be traced back to antiquity.

The nomadic peoples not only wove kilims. In fact, a large proportion of the finest Tribal Rugs to be found are knotted carpets, but not the thick, unwieldy rugs that we often associate with Oriental rugs. Their designs are similar to the ones found in kilims, geometric with abstracted animal and floral details. These pile rugs were made primarily for sale and trade, kilims were made for home use. All the weavings that the nomadic women would make were utilitarian. They may have served as trappings for horses or containers for cooking utensils, or wraps for precious objects such as a family's copy of the Koran. Flat-woven rugs could be folded and stacked for easy transport from one encampment to the next. Every aspect of nomadic life had to be fluid. A kilim was your bed cover, your table, your overcoat on a cold night. Bags that were made to carry the tent walls were later used as a storage bag for rice and wheat. They were hung horizontally around the tent to provide insulation as well as color, and over the entranceway as a door.

For the nomadic people, what was considered comfort in Europe was discomfort for them. They didn't carry chairs and tables from camp to camp. Instead they created textiles that could serve all the multi-functional needs that they had.

About Nomadic Life

Contrary to most peoples perception of nomadic life, the tribes people do not wander aimlessly through the countryside. In actuality, the life of a nomad is very precise and highly structured.

Dating back to prehistory, there are indications that scattered, isolated shepherd families grouped together in order to move their large flocks of animals for summer and winter grazing. Safety in numbers, one assumes. These groups consequently became highly organized. Systems for allotting pasture rights evolved and strong leaders known as "Khans" emerged. Many of the Khans became tyrants — Atilla and Gengis Khan to name the two best known. Ultimately, they played the role of negotiators between the tribes people and the central governments. They had tremendous power amongst the tribes, collecting taxes, conscripting warriors, and providing and limiting pasture rights during the spring and summer grazing. A weak Khan was of little use to the government and, on the other hand, a Khan who was too strong would ultimately become a threat. Nowadays, even though most Khans are highly educated and keep abreast of modern life, they do not wield enough power to protect their people's way of life.

Self sufficiency was the main aspect of nomadic life, but this never precluded economic support from towns and cities, which provided markets for wool and livestock. In truth, being part of a nomadic tribe did not always imply a year-round nomadic life; millions of nomads live in villages for part of the year or even permanently without forsaking their tribal identities.

Migratory groups, however, move purposefully to find favorable conditions for their animals at least twice a year. The same animals that dictate the nomads life also provided for his lifestyle. Sheep and goats provide dairy products and meat and their skins are used for clothes, shoes, and shelter. Camels and horses were once the primary means of transportation, but these days four-wheel drive trucks can be found in the most isolated areas.

The routes that the tribes traveled became dotted with small villages and semi-permanent dwellings to meet the needs of nomads passing through. I have been to villages where everyone's occupation is connected to "The Rug Trade." Villages with a plentiful water supply became centers for washing, shearing, spinning, and dying. Larger towns and cities, especially oasis, became market centers for buying and selling finished rugs. Some of these towns lend their names to nomadic rugs, such as Zarands, Maiminas, and Ardibiles — all these terms Western dealers use to identify certain rugs are actually the names of towns, not the identity of the weavers who produced them.

Existence has always been difficult for minorities in Central Asia. Nowadays news coverage of ethnic cleansing and full-scale wars against such minorities has brought their plight to the full attention of the West, but for nomadic people it has been part of their existence for hundreds of years. The fact that we can still locate such groups is a miracle, and that they have preserved their traditions and way of life is even more surprising. I always feel when you buy a traditional textile from this part of the world, whether old or new, that you are buying a little piece of their strength and perseverance as well.

About the Rugs

Generally kilims are made of one-hundred percent wool, the flocks of sheep and goats being a nomad's most important resource.

The men are responsible for shearing and dying and the women spin the wool and weave the rugs. Until I spent time amongst tribal people, I assumed that weaving traditions were passed from mothers to daughters, but in fact the skill and the traditional patterns jumps from grandmothers to granddaughters. The wife and mother being far too busy running all the aspects of daily life to actually do much of the teaching, although she will also weave. Children start weaving at a very young age. A woman is still expected to contribute to her dowry by producing a number of rugs and, of course, her skill is considered when the marriage contract is negotiated. It is not true, however, that all tribal women are weavers, and it is not the case that all weavers are skilled artisans. Even though the tribal people do not consider weaving an art form, the reputation of a fine craftswomen will spread far beyond her tribal group. I have tracked down such fabled weavers, usually to be met by an ancient matriarch who, despite her modesty, compels respect from even the most swaggering young men of the tribe.

The quality of the wool, of course, effects the finished product, which is why we find such enormous differences between rugs from different areas. The richer the grazing lands, the better the quality of the wool. The breed of the sheep also determines the quality of wool produced. Sheep have been domesticated in Asia for thousands of years. The fat-tailed sheep is the most common breed. These sheep have huge, pendulous tails that often weigh thirty pounds and sustain the animal in dry, inhospitable environments. Their wool produces a hard, lustrous yarn of excellent dye-taking quality. In the higher mountains, the fleece is finer and more luxuriant than the wool from the plains, where the land is arid, hot, and dusty. Unlike their American relatives, Asian sheep are multi-colored and often their wool is carded and sorted into colors before any dying begins. If the natural color is rich and attractive it is often left un-dyed, giving us the rich browns and soft creamy colors so often found in Tribal pieces.

Spinning is done by hand, and even though it's considered women's work, it is such a laborious task that most of the family will pitch in. It's a common sight to see young and old, men and women, spinning yarn while doing some other job at the same time. The tools are simple, lightweight spindles and each tribal group has its own distinctive design. It wasn't until we started producing kilims that we understood the importance of hand spinning, which gives the yarn a rough, slightly spiked texture essential in producing a tightly packed, fine weave. Machine-spun wool, we discovered, was too shiny, making the weave bulky and loose.

Most of the looms are very simple in their design. If the group is still migratory, the loom will be a horizontal structure, close to the ground. Its design makes it easy to dismantle and transport on the back of an animal, usually with a half-finished rug on board. In the settled communities of towns and villages, vertical-framed looms are mainly used. These are much larger and wider structures that allow weavers to make large-sized, one-piece rugs.

There is and always will be controversy about natural and aniline dyes. Natural dyes are generally preferred, but aniline dyes can be found in many extremely expensive antique pieces. In 1850, an Englishman called W. Perkins started a color revolution by inventing aniline dye from coal tar. Up until then the status of the dyers was extremely high. Their secrets and skills made them famous and powerful throughout the ancient world, and they guarded their recipes, often taking them to the grave. Mr. Perkins changed all that. Weavers who had been limited in their choice of colors suddenly had the spectrum of a rainbow to choose from. Certain colors like orange and yellow, which had been hard to fix, were now easy to use. New dyes were less expensive and easier to produce. The use of chemical colors rapidly spread, even to the most isolated and self sufficient tribal weavers. Most tribal rugs produced since then are a combination of chemical and natural dyes, but in the past decade the lobby for natural dyes seems to have the upper edge again as many producers in Turkey and Pakistan have started reviving the old techniques.

Every dye, natural and chemical, needs to be fixed by using some type of mordant. Mordants, from the Latin word to bite, does exactly that. The yarn is soaked in a solution that penetrates the wool so the dye can take. Ancient mordants included solutions of roots, urine, and fruits. Today solutions of caustic soda and slaked lime are usually used.

Even though dyes became sophisticated, the techniques for dying remained primitive. Most yarn is vat dyed, which means the yarn is thrown into large pots of prepared liquid dye. I've passed through villages on the migratory trails where you see men with indigo, red, and orange arms because they throw the skeins of wool into huge vats and, after the appointed time, reach in and pull them out.

Very few weavers will actually dye their own wool. Their wool will be spun and stored until they pass through one of these towns where it will be either dyed to their request or traded for already dyed yarn. In many of the nomadic rugs you will find vast changes of color throughout the rug because only small quantities of yarn were available every shearing season. This is one of the characteristics I love about tribal pieces, and in the rugs from the early seventies and eighties you often find small areas of fluorescent colors. I like to believe these are a legacy from the castoff sweaters of the hippies that passed through on their journeys to enlightenment, but it is more likely to be imported dyes from India or China.

The shape of kilims is often very difficult to understand; they tend to be long and quite narrow. This had a lot to do with the looms the weavers used, but even more, I believe, with the architecture of the region. In this part of the world you don't find too many forests. In fact, wood is a very precious commodity and, until the advent of steel and cement, it was very unusual to find houses with large rectangular rooms. Most houses were long and thin. A large house would be a warren of such buildings, the more simple dwelling just one narrow room. So the long, skinny proportions of kilims were perfect. Since there was no market in Europe for kilims until the later half of the nineteenth century, by the simple logic of demand, very few Western-sized kilims were made. Of course, there are always exceptions to the rule and certain tribal groups produced large pieces, either for ceremonial occasions like weddings and sometimes as gifts from wealthy families to the local mosques. Many other shapes of kilims were produced such as squares and small rectangles to be used for eating mats, larger oblong pieces for door hangings and prayer rugs. Generally speaking, however, a kilim is an odd-shaped rug, which has been one of the problems for designers and buyers. But with a little imagination, a perfect spot can usually be found.

About the Value

If you are interested in buying a rug as an investment, I honestly believe that buying a kilim is the best choice for you. I have already mentioned that, until quite recently, kilims were not considered very desirable floor coverings in the western world. Their odd proportions, bright colors, and strong geometric designs were appreciated by only a handful of people, who often became passionate collectors. For years, when I would arrive in a market looking for kilims, a dusty pile would be hauled out from the far corner of the shop. Some of the pieces were hundreds of years old. I would always ask the dealer the origin and age of these kilims and, in many cases, they would have no idea. Sometimes they would admit that their fathers or grandfathers had bought them. They did not value them in the same way as the knotted pile rugs. Supply and demand creates the going rate, after all. It's not quite so easy nowadays, but beautiful old kilims can still be found at affordable prices. I can testify that the value of these rugs does increase.

One question I'm often asked is how you can tell the age of a carpet? You should find a dealer who you trust and ask them to show you both old and new rugs. It is really only direct experience that will help you with this problem.

There are, however, a few things to look for that will help you determine whether the rug is old or new:

* Check out the symbols and the motifs. If you see something that looks like a tank or a airplane, the chances are the rug was made quite recently. A rug of any age will usually have some repair, which won't necessarily devalue the rug. It is very exceptional to find an antique piece without at least some repair at its edges or fringe.

* Check both sides of the rug, quite often a rug will be faded and old on one side and considerably brighter on the other. This usually means that the manufacturer has put the rug out to fade. I have passed through miles and miles of countryside with fields of rugs all fading in the bright Eastern sunshine.

* Smell the rug too. Nowadays, chemicals are used to wash the rugs. Called "tea dying" or "antique washed" the process leaves behind a strong acrid smell.

* Also, beware of the pricing. There are not many dealers who don't know the market value of kilims; if the price seems too good to be true, it probably is.

So go out there, hunt, and may the force be with you.

THE KILIMS OF PERSIA

This huge area of southwestern Asia is, and always has been, the home of hundreds of tribal and nomadic people. It is now known again by its ancient name Iran. This region was described by the conqueror Marco Polo as a great land, the greatness referring to its crafts as well as its empire. From the eighteenth century onward, Persian Rugs became a symbol of wealth, fine large carpets, woven with intricate designs and sophisticated color patterns. They were commissioned and exported to the West by the thousands. The influence of such a huge trade did have some effect on the nomadic people, but it is only recently that interest has been shown by the western world in their distinctive, highly colored flatweaves..

The kilims from this region vary enormously, and modern Iran comprised of many tribal groups of varied origins.

Two of the earliest indigenous tribes, the Kurds and the Lurs, are still very active in Iran. The Kurds, the long-time inhabitants of northern Iran, were probably the first people to develop the art of weaving kilims. As the oldest indigenous group, their history is laced with folklore. King Solomon with his army of supernatural "Jinns," is reputed to be their forefather. The king sent his supernatural warriors off to the West to find five hundred beautiful virgins to add to his harem. Unfortunately, so the story goes, Solomon died before the army returned, so the Jinns married their prizes. Thus the origin of the Kurdish nation.

History has not been so generous to the Kurds. Constant political maneuvering by their chiefs, the redrawing of international frontiers, and forced migrations have assimilated the ancient Kurds into peoples of different nationalities and beliefs, but their language, although in many different dialects, still unites them as one people.

Large communities of Kurds can be found in northeastern Iran, parts of Turkestan, and to a smaller extent in Southern Iran. Beyond the border of Iran, groups of Kurds can be found in Syria, Turkey, and northeastern Iraq.

As the Kurds are so widely spread, it's not surprising that their kilims differ from each other in design, colors, structure, and size. They range from the sophisticated workshop-made kilims of Senna to highly individual tribal rugs woven on crude ground looms with coarsely spun wool. Designs can range from rugs carved with delicate florals from the town workshops to quirky representations of animals and humans.

The best way to proceed now is to show you some examples of Kurdish rugs that I have in stock and in my private collection. The pieces I own have not necessarily been chosen for their value. In fact the opposite is probably more the truth, the valuable pieces are always for sale. I have made my choice, as I hope you do, on aesthetic judgment and that little ping in the heart when you first spot the rug of your dreams.

I'm going to start first with two groups of rugs known as Zarand and Bijar. They are both generic names given because of the towns in which they are traded. These kilims are very similar and easily confused. In fact, in many cases my categorizations are little more than educated guesses.

Zarand and Bijar

Zarand is a town to the southwest of Tehran. The name not only covers the textiles of Zarand itself, but also the Qazvin and Saveh regions to the north. The nomads who wove the rugs were descendants of a Turkic-speaking people called Shahsavan. They were based in northwestern Persia, but moved freely across most of Central Asia.

These rugs were often bypassed by dealers in the first half of the twentieth century, because of their usual use of color and combination of aniline and natural dyes. You will see from the following photgraphs that quite often a rug will change color dramatically from one end to the other.

These pieces are personal favorites for me, reminding me of the patchwork quilts found here in America and the old rag rugs of Europe. You definitely get the feeling that every bit of available yarn has been used and, even though these weavers have never seen a painting from the French Impressionist movement, the finished rugs often resemble a Monet or a Manet.

Zarand kilims are long and narrow and extremely durable. They have a warp thread (the thread that runs vertically) of cotton, and a weft thread (that runs horizontally) of thick durable wool. They are always woven using the slit-weave technique.

There are three major designs to be found in these pieces: a repeating spider motif, a small abstracted flower design, and an even smaller repeated motif I affectionately call "packman." It is the small all-over central field that makes these pieces so attractive. It also shows us that these very primitive weavers were heavily influenced by the sophisticated weavers of Sanandaj, the capital of Kurdistan, where Senna rugs and kilims were produced.

There are also two very distinctive colorways to be found in these kilims. One being very muted and soft, the other bright and bold. It is hard to say why one family would use muted tones and the other bright, possibly just personal preference.

Bijar, a word that actually means 'mixing of people' is a market town on the edge of Kurdistan. These pieces originate from the town and dozens of surrounding villages. As I said, Bijar kilims are often confused with Zarands, but the appearance of animals and human figures found in Bijars differentiate them. These figures are often woven on each side of the rug and depict married couples,

Bijar. This kilim is from my private collection. I love it. It is a great example of a Bijar. The colors are bright and joyful, the spider motif runs down it's center, but what makes this piece unique are the multitude of figures crowding the central "guls." Quite often the lives of the nomadic weavers are reflected in their designs and this one is obviously a family portrait. A combination of aniline and natural dies. 9' x 3'2". Circa 1940s. Private Collection.

their children, their families, and flocks. Kilims decorated in this fashion were probably made for weddings and dowries by young women. They are typically long and narrow with bold patterns of medallions; usually with two borders.

Unfortunately both the Zarands and the Bijars that you see here are among the last to be had. These nomadic peoples were forced into resettlement programs and now produce naive copies of Senna kilims and the far more commercial knotted carpets for export.

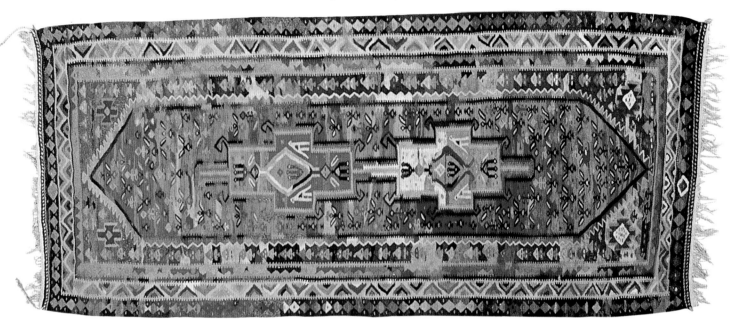

Above: Bijar. This is a prayer rug. We can tell this by its size and also its design. Prayer rugs are very personal objects for these weavers and this one is a fine example of their use of color and symbolic designs. 6' x 3'. Value: $2,000.

Left: Closeup of central gul.

Detail of border. This symbol appears often in these Kurdish
kilims. It appears to be an eye, which is a symbol of protection.

A corner detail. Note the two borders, with the outer one
showing the distinctive "laleh abrassi" or tulip design.

This piece is also from my private collection. It's from the 1940s and, although it's full of figures, its overall appearance pegs it as a Zarand. Note the wonderful, subtle color changes occurring throughout this rug. The dyes are natural. 9' x 3'. $2,000-2,500.

Zarand. This is a great example of how weavers would work small areas of a rug from one dye lot and resume weaving when more materials were available. When first made, the weavers would try and match the dyes, but as the rug has aged, some color lots faded more quickly, giving the present day rug this very attractive abrash. Small motifs form a diamond pattern throughout the rug. Circa mid-1940s-'50s. 9' x 3'. $1,800.

Detail showing how dye lots differed.

Detail of diamond pattern.

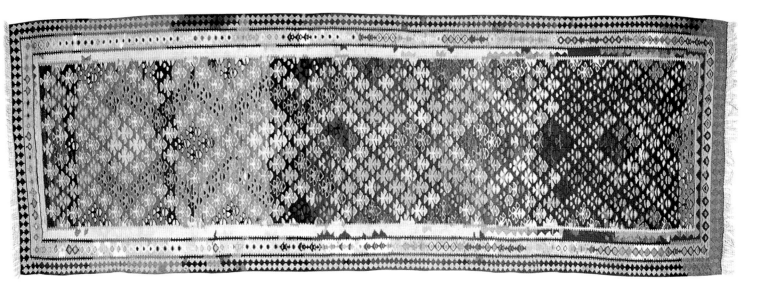

Kurdish Zarand. This is a perfect example of the small designs found in these rugs. It shows the skill of these Kurdish weavers. Circa 1940s. $1,800.

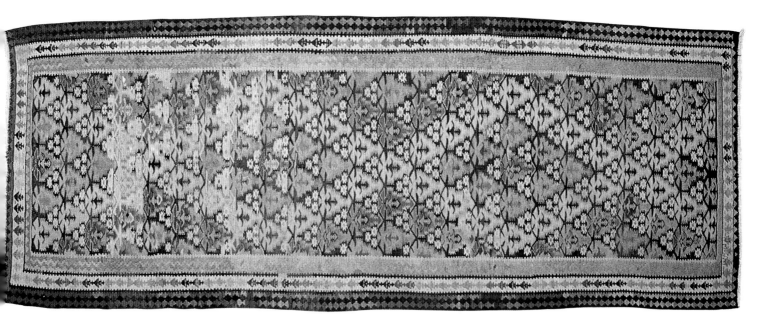

Zarand. This rug is a combination of vegetable dyes and wool. Sheep in this part of the world are multi-colored and quite often the yarn was simply washed and spun and then woven directly into the rug. 8'10" x 3'7". $1,500.

Above: Zarand. You can really see the natural wool colors in this rug. It's interesting because the central field is comprised of a double row of medallions., maybe formatted to fit this particular rug's dimensions. Circa 1930s-1940s. $1,700.

Below: Detail shows the double medallions. Note the color variations in the natural browns, and the use of mulberry dyes for a purple hue.

Above: The major differences between the rugs from the 1930's and the '60s can be seen in this piece. The wool is not as fine and there is more use of aniline dyes, yet the design and the feel of the rug is the same. Circa 1950-'60. $1,200.

Left: Zarand. This piece is interesting because of the double motif in the central field. Its colors are bright and lively. A really joyful rug. 1950-'60. 9'3" x 3'2". $1,200.

Zarand. This piece is full of great colors. It's almost like
a patchwork quilt. Circa 1960. 8'10" x 3'4". $1,200.

This is a great
example of the
abstracted eye. The
Muslim weavers are
very superstitious
about eyes. Blue
eyes, being very rare
in the Middle East,
have great power.
They are supposed
to reflect evil
(something that has
always been to my
advantage).

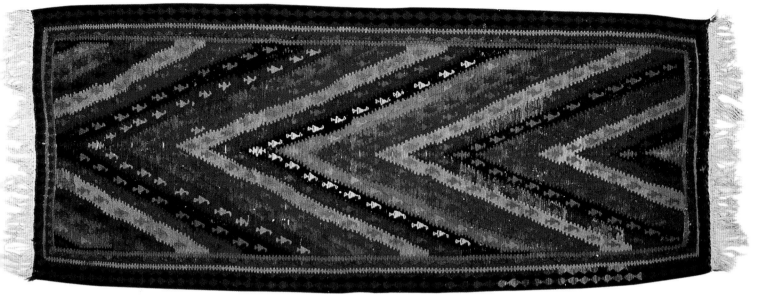

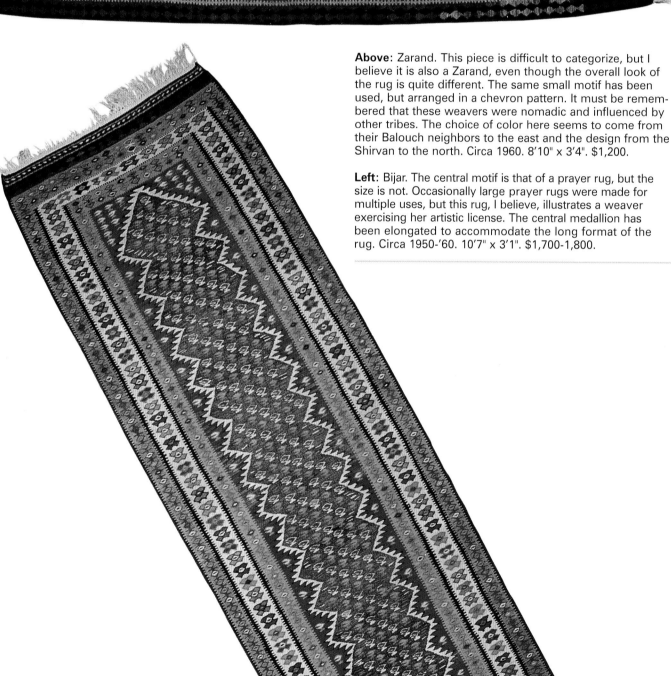

Above: Zarand. This piece is difficult to categorize, but I believe it is also a Zarand, even though the overall look of the rug is quite different. The same small motif has been used, but arranged in a chevron pattern. It must be remembered that these weavers were nomadic and influenced by other tribes. The choice of color here seems to come from their Balouch neighbors to the east and the design from the Shirvan to the north. Circa 1960. 8'10" x 3'4". $1,200.

Left: Bijar. The central motif is that of a prayer rug, but the size is not. Occasionally large prayer rugs were made for multiple uses, but this rug, I believe, illustrates a weaver exercising her artistic license. The central medallion has been elongated to accommodate the long format of the rug. Circa 1950-'60. 10'7" x 3'1". $1,700-1,800.

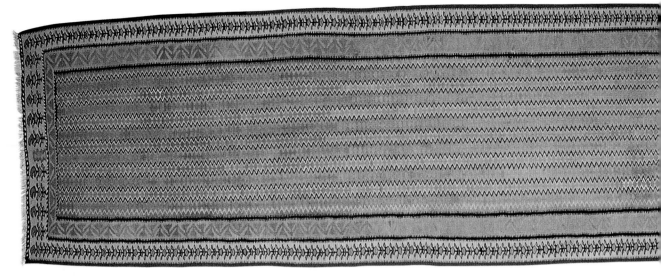

Bijar. In all the years I've been buying a selling rugs, I've never found one in this design before. The size is also very unusual, which leads me to believe it might have been custom-made. I'm going to put it with the Bijar's because of the thick, coarsely spun wool. Pre-1950. 10'11 x 3'7. $2,500.

Zarand. This pattern, which looks like fall trees, is very common in Kurdish rugs and has been attributed to the Zarands. This example is unusual because of its width. 10'5" x 4'4". $2,500.

Bijar. This piece could be attributed to the Shahsavan. Its color and the thickness of the yarn defines it as Kurdish and certainly from the Bijar region. Circa 1950s. 10'11" x 3'9". $1,500.

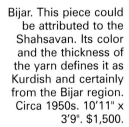

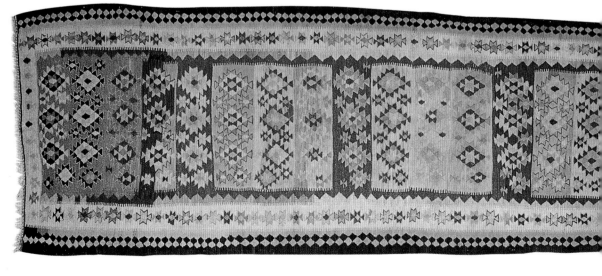

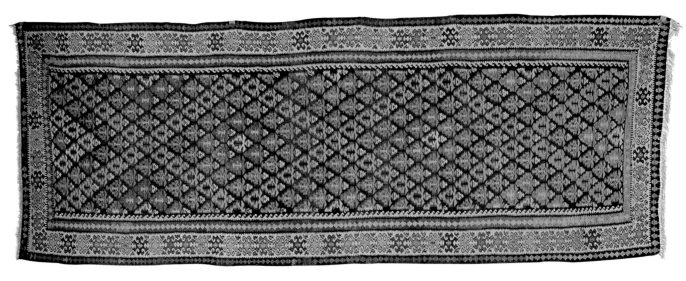

Zarand. This kilim has an overall tree-like pattern.

A detail of a very interesting border. This piece displays obvious influence from the kilims of the Caucuses. The symbols used are typical of Shirvan kilims. 1950s. 10'2" x 3'8". $1,800.

A Bijar kilim using the
classical Shahsavan
banded design. 1940s-
50s. $1,700-1,800.

Above: Zarand. An early 20th Century Zarand. Especially large, this was probably made for ceremonial use. 14'6" x 4'9". $4,000.

Below: Note the similarities to Senna motifs, shown in the following section.

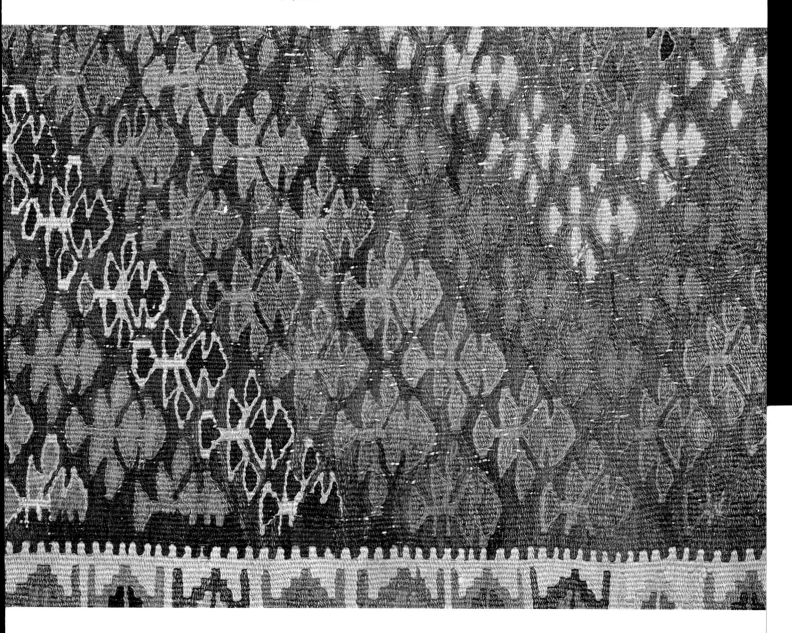

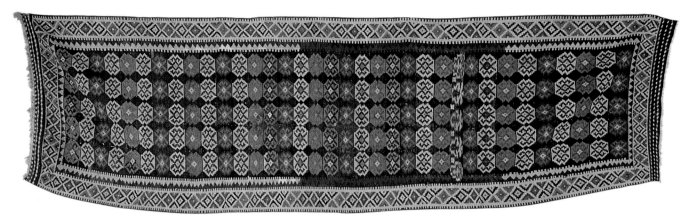

Bijar. A Kurdish piece that uses many different
motifs. 1940-50. 13' x 3'9". $2,000-2,500.

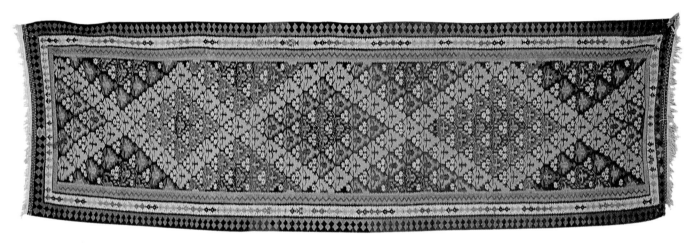

Zarand. A beautiful example of a Kurdish Zarand, with
the diamond motif running the length of the rug.
1930-40. 11'8 x 3'4'. $2,000.

Bijar. A lovely example of a Kurdish rug. Shows dye-lot
changes and the balanced, traditional diamond pattern so
typical of these pieces. 1940s. 12'6" x 3'8". $1,500-1,800.

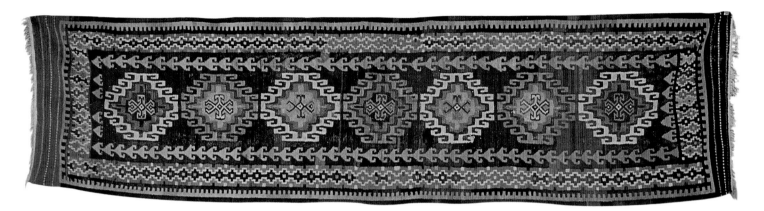

Bijar. A combination of natural dyes and unbleached wool.
Note the wonderful multi-borders which are typical of these
pieces. 1940s. 13'9" x 3'6". $1,500-1,800.

Talish. A Kurdish piece with a lovely all-over diamond motif. This
piece features the bright, clear colors used in the northwest of Iran.
It uses a simple diamond design demanded by its slit-weave
technique. Its colors are strong enough to match the strength of its
design. This piece shows the characteristics of the Talish area of
Iran, on the shores of the Caspian Sea. 1940-50. $1,800-2,000.

Above: Bijar. This is full of wonderful details of animals and people. Animal figures portray the importance of owning a herd of sheep. It indicates the wealth of the tribe. This piece has a very unusual use of color. 1950s. 9' x 3'. Private collection.

Right & opposite: Detail shots of figures. Note the great abstraction of birds and people in this rug. The side borders are especially detailed.

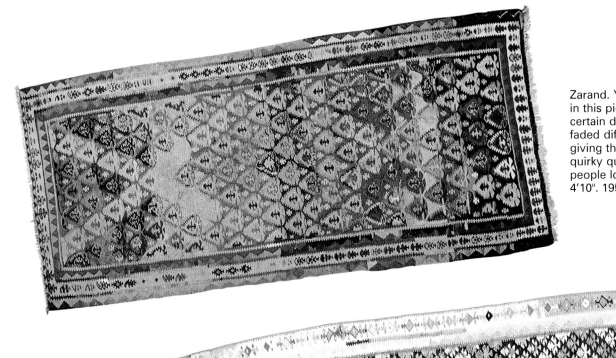

Zarand. You can see in this piece how certain dye lots have faded differently, giving this rug the quirky quality many people love. 8'3" x 4'10". 1950s. $1,800.

Zarand. A good example of the use of both cotton and wool. Cotton was used to give dramatic contrast to the darker hues of the unbleached yarn. This piece is both peaceful and dynamic at the same time. 8' x 4'. 1950s. $1,200-1,500.

Zarand. This is a beautiful piece from the early 20th Century. It's a fabulous example of how these weavers had small quantities of different dye lots and created a patchwork quilt effect. 7'7" x 3'3". $1,800-2,000.

Zarand. This piece is a great example of the color changes that occur in these rugs. It is a finely woven piece in the stepped slit-weave technique. 1930-40. 9' x 3'3". $1,800-2,000.

Kurdish. This rug is hard to classify. It is strongly influenced by weavings from the southern Caucuses, but its use of cotton for the warp threads and its running border inclines me to place it as a Kurdish piece, almost definitely from northwestern Iran. I can't stress enough how much these people were influenced by the areas to which they traveled. 1950s-'60s. 9'6" x 4'. $1,200-1,500.

Above: A Kurdish piece from the far north of Iran. It's a peculiar piece because it almost takes on the effect of an eye dazzler. Very atypical. A combination of natural and aniline dyes. A bold piece. 1950s. 10'4" x 3'10". $1,200-1,500.

Right: Zarand with wonderful leaf border. The colors in this piece indicate that it is a slightly more modern piece. Its central field design is certainly Zarand, but the texture of the wool suggests a Bijar and the border a Senna. The one thing we know for sure is that it's a great Kurdish piece. Circa 1960. 9'1" x 3'2". $1,800.

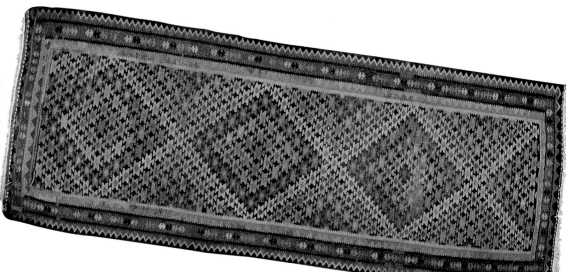

Kurdish Zarand. A great example of the small flower bud motif, arranged diagonally to form diamond medallions throughout the central field. 1950s. 8'11" x 3'5". $1,500.

Kurdish. This rug's unusual color and design lead me to believe that its weavers had been to Daghestan, where the same large abstract motifs, known as "rukzals" are used. The coarseness of the yarn and the weaving technique are certainly Kurdish. A great example of cross-cultural influences. 1960s. 10'7" x 4'1". $1,200.

Kurdish Zarand. The use of green in this piece makes it both an unusual and an exciting rug. Here white cotton has been used instead of wool to enhance the brightness of the greens and reds. Circa 1940s. 8'2" x 2'10". $1,800.

Above: Kurdish Zarand. Nicely drawn rug in pale, subtle colors. Not very old and lacking a bit of the spontaneity of its ancestors. 8'10" x 3'7". Circa 1970. $1,000.

Left: Kurdish. This rug has an unusually large, strong design, probably influenced by the Kuba weavers of Georgia. Its coloration doesn't help us too much either, neither being typical of a Bijar or a Kuba. Its width and the fineness of the weave indicates it's from one of the village workshops in northwestern Iran. Circa 1950. 10'7" x 4'. $1,200.

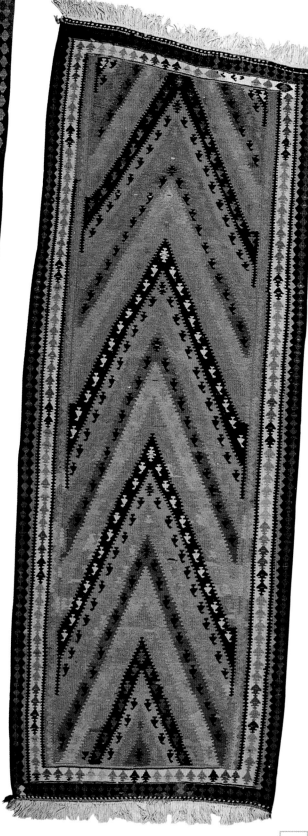

Above: Zarand. A more modern piece using rich purples and orange. The double row of medallions gives it a rich, full look. Pieces like this work well in heavily used areas of the home, and will fade nicely throughout the years. Circa 1970. 9'2" x 3'4". $1,000.

Right: Zarand. An unusual piece because of the use of the chevron design. 9'7" x 3'9". Circa 1950s. $1,200.

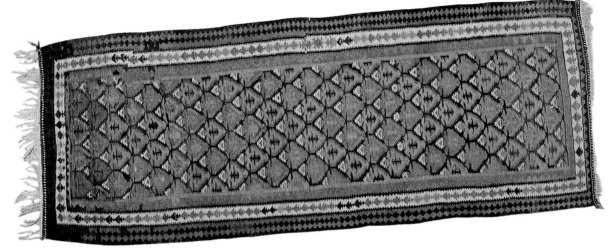

Zarand. A great rug for lovers of the color orange. This piece, though of little age, is vibrant and happy. Pieces from this period were made from vat dyed yarn and will fade nicely throughout the years. This is an antique rug in progress, and a good investment. 9'5" x 3'6". Circa 1960. $1,000.

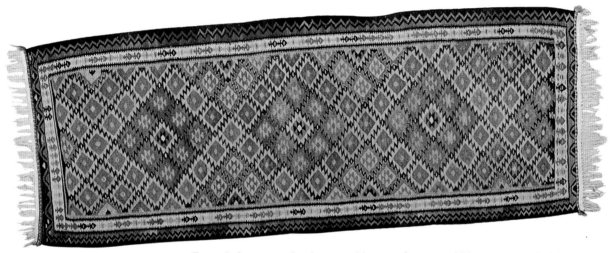

Zarand. An unusual colorway, this rug of gray and blues was probably influenced by western tastes. This piece is a great example of how the Kurds of Zarand carefully arrange small motifs diagonally to create large diamond patterns in the field of the rug. 9'4" x 3'6". Circa 1960. $1,200.

Bijar. A great example of the all-over diamond pattern. This rug uses unbleached yarn and very soft natural dyed yarn. If the natural tones of the yarn were attractive, they did not dye it. The rather coarse wefts indicate its origins rather than its design. Circa 1950. 9'1" x 3'3". $1,500.

Above: Zarand. This rug has a lovely leaf border similar to the intricate borders of the Senna Rugs. Its colors are soft. The effect was achieved by using natural dyes and unbleached wool. Circa 1960s. 9'3" x 3'4". $1,200.

Left: A lovely, long runner with a strong, defined pattern. Note the running border that echoes the central medalions. Circa 1960. 10'7" x 3'. $1,200.

Right: Kurdish, possibly from the Talish area. This rug displays an obvious Caucasian influence. Its clear bright colors and its white diamond border distinguish it from its neighbors, the Shahsavan. 11'5" x 3'3". $2,500

Below: Kurdish Talish. The color of this piece is very unusual, but its distinctive diagonal inner border places it from this area. Circa 1960s. 10'3" x 3'3". $1,500.

Above: This is a very modern piece using harsh orange and purple dyes. It is a nicely written rug and very well woven. One has to wonder who provided such unsympathetic colors, probably a commercial dealer in Tehran. These pieces do have some appeal, but lack the spontaneity of older pieces. Circa 1970s. 9'4" x 3'5". $650.

Right: Bijar. This rug, with its strong diamond design, emphasizes how Bijar is the weaving center for many tribes. This kilim could be attributed to many tribes from northwest Iran, but its weave and yarn places it as a Kurdish piece. Its coloration dates it from the late '60s. 9'6" x 3'4". $1,000.

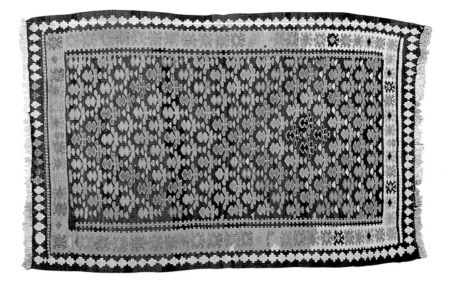

Above: Zarand. The length of this rug makes it quite unusual. This piece could have been made for use in the local mosque or commissioned by a family for a specific space. Circa 1950. 11'7" x 3'3". $1,800.

Right: Zarand. Extremely small piece using both wool and cotton. Great execution here of the small motif creating large medallions. Even though this rug does not have a typical prayer rug design, the small dark medallion at one end makes me believe that this was placed pointing to Mecca. Circa 1940s. 5' x 3'4". $1,800.

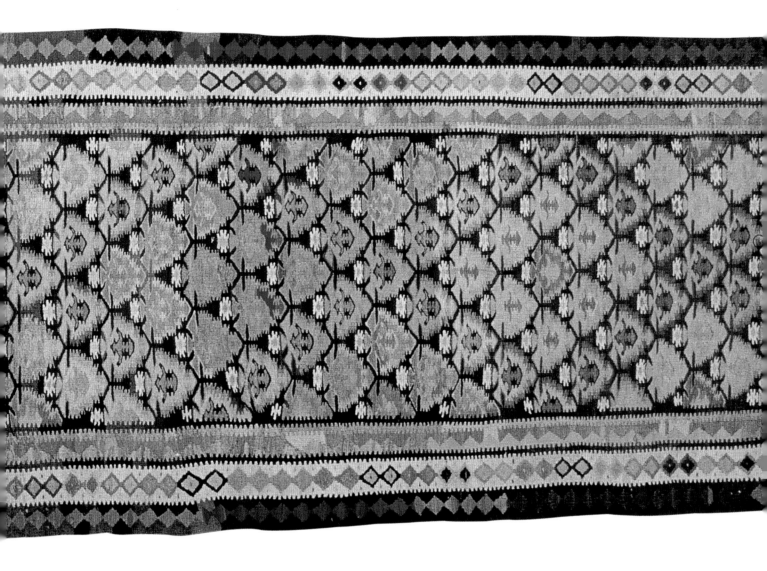

Zarand. The central field of this piece is a lovely repeat of diamond patterns. It has a wonderful bright patchwork quilt effect. Circa 1940. 8'8" x 3'4". $1,800.

Above: Zarand. A great example of the small motif arranged diagonally to create large medallions in the central field. Circa 1960. 8'8" x 3'1". $1,200.

Right: Kurdish Zarand. Circa 1960. 9'3" x 3'9". $1,000.

Above: Kurdish. This rug has a wonderful indigo blue ground and a central field of diamonds. It is very reminiscent of a rug from Azerbaijan. The rows of narrow borders are typical of that area in northwestern Iran. The best I can say about this piece is that it's definitely from that region. Circa 1950. 10'2" x 4'2". $1,500.

Left: Kurdish Talish. This piece has an usual combination of reds, yellows, and blues. Its interlocking diamond pattern suggests it could be from the Caspian Sea area of Talish. 10'10" x 3'8".

Zarand. Great use of bright, vibrant blues with a wonderful multiple border. Circa 1960. 10'2" x 3'6". $1,500.

Bijar. This piece has a great indigo blue ground and a very defined ivory wool border. 1960s. $1,200.

Bijar. This rug is difficult to categorize because its central field is not typical. The texture of the wool suggests Bijar as its origin. 1960s. $1,200.

Kurdish. Heavily influenced by Caucasian weavers, this rug is probably from Northern Iran. Great all-over diamond design. Circa 1950. $1,500.

Bijar. Great example of the running diamond motif found in Bijar pieces. Very finely woven in the double interlock technique. 1950s. $2,000.

Above: Bijar. This rug has a wonderfully defined diamond pattern. Its borders are reminiscent of Shirvan rugs.

Below: Note the wonderful running border.

About The Senna

Senna kilims are also Kurdish, and are another rug named after the town where they are produced. This village, now called Sanandaj is the capital of Kurdistan in Iran. Fine-quality carpets and kilims are still being made there today.

Senna kilims are totally different, both technically and aesthetically, from the bold nomadic kilims woven elsewhere by the Kurdish tribes. The Senna weavers were strongly influenced by the floral patterns of the Safavid embroidery, which was, in turn, influenced by Indian textiles exported from Kashmir in the nineteenth century.

Craftsmanship and technical skill is far more important to these weavers than overall design. They use a slit weave, which they have refined by using extra weft inserts and curved wefts. This means they can have a curvilinear outline with no jagged steps or breaks in the pattern. The colors are rich blues and ivory.

There's a lot of myth about the old Sennas, that they were used as room dividers in the harems and that every wife wanted to make a more intricate one than the wife to follow. Whether this was true or not, these are definitely some of the finest flat-woven rugs that you can find.

These rugs were well cared for as they were considered a status symbol. Many fine early pieces have survived.

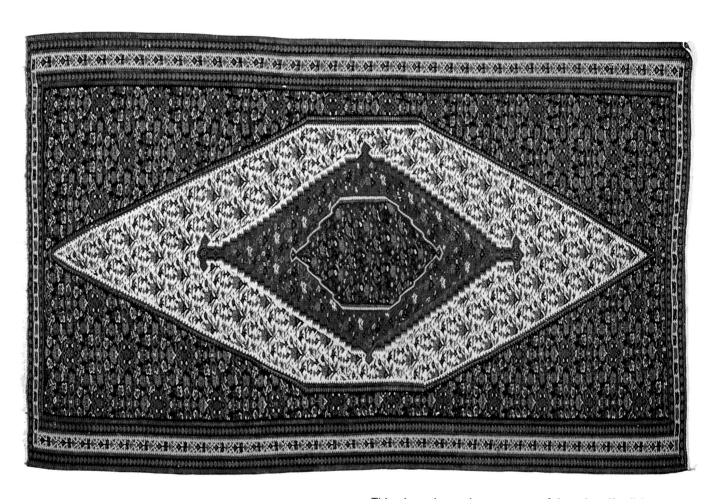

This piece shows the greatness of the urban Kurdish weavers from Senna. The central medallion is similar to the formal carpets of Persia. Early 20th Century. $4,500.

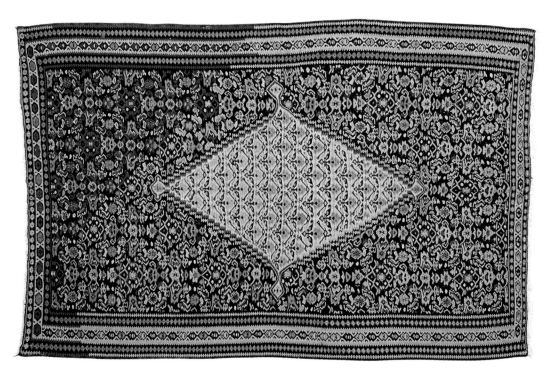

Right: This piece was not made in one of the urban workshops. It is far too eccentric for that. Note the change of yarn in the top left-hand side of the rug. This indicates some nomadic influence or, at least, a very small workshop. Very old, late 19th Century. 6'9" x 4'4". $6,000.

Below: The borders of this piece are of interlocking vines and flowers. Note the richness of color and the fineness of the weave.

The Kurds of Khorassan (Quchan)

Khorassan means the land of the rising sun. It is a wonderful, rich fertile area of Iran. Meshad is now the major city of the region, just across the Iranian border with Afghanistan. Meshad is the only place in the world I have worn chadre, in order to enter the main mosque where the most beautiful collections of rugs are displayed. It was, strangely, quite a liberating experience, but I was thankful to be able to remove this unpleasant garment when I chose to. Anyone who traveled overland from west to east during the '60s and '70s knows this wonderful city full of ancient mosques and narrow lanes.

This particular group of weavings are made by semi-nomadic Kurds living around the market town of Quchan, which has subsequently given its name to this type of kilim. I used to travel frequently to this area and at one time had a huge collection of their work, but alas political troubles have closed that border to me.

Their flatweaves are wide and incorporate a rich variety of techniques and colors. It is possible to trace some of their motifs back to their Caucasian and even Anatolian ancestors. Many motifs are similar to those of the Balouch and often are mistaken as such.

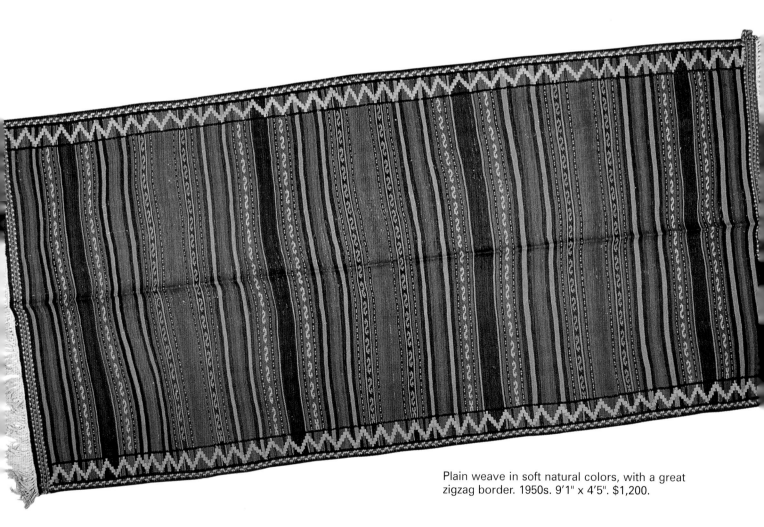

Plain weave in soft natural colors, with a great zigzag border. 1950s. 9'1" x 4'5". $1,200.

Above: Note the wonderful bright colors and the intricate motifs. ". 1960s-'70s. 10' x 5'1. $500-600.

Right: Detail of Quchan showing the elaborate weft patterning so artfully employed by these weavers.

Here the weave is weft wrapping loosely worked. The colors are rather subdued. 1950s. 9'10" x 5'1". $1,500.

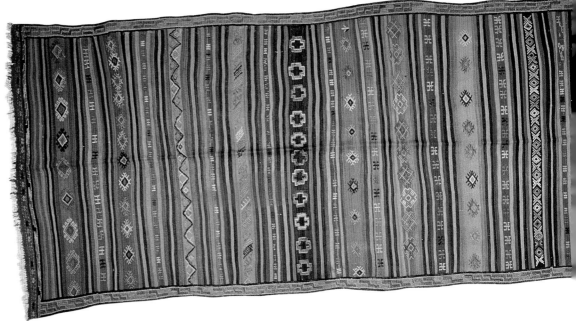

Above: This rug reminds me of the amazing sunsets in Khorassan. This is one piece I managed to keep for myself. 1950s. 9'2" x 4'5".

Left: Note the motif, which is similar to rugs from the Caucuses.

The Lurs and The Qashqai

The Lurs are one of the few tribal groups who still live in their native land. They are to be found in southwestern Iran, from the Iraq-Iran border to the Gulf plateau near Shiraz. Not much is known about their history, apart from the fact that they manufactured the famous Luristan Bronzes in the fifth and sixth centuries BC. These small bronze sculptures are the earliest surviving examples of nomadic art. They are small figurines, made as horse bits and harness decorations. The same two-headed or multi-headed animal symbols can be found in weavings from this area today.

They managed to exist unchanged for so long, perhaps because of the remoteness of their land. This part of Iran is very isolated, a land of rugged mountains and inhospitable desert. Unfortunately, the discovery of oil and the improvement of communications and transportation in the twentieth century has changed their traditional lifestyle. Their independence ended with Reza Shah's enforced settlement program in the late 1930s.

Their designs are quite different from their neighbors, the Kurds and other Turkic speaking tribes. Some believe that their designs originated from the fifth and sixth century BC, from the same culture that produced the famous Luristan Bronzes.

The Qashqai and Lurs are tribal neighbors, but their rugs differ significantly. The wool of Luri kilims is loosely spun and quite coarse whereas that of the Qashqai are softer and more lustrous.

For centuries, most rugs from Southern Iran were known collectively as Shiraz. This name derives from a large central town in this area that was famous in the 17th and 18th centuries for weaving and is now a large market town.

Like all the tribal people of Persia, the Lurs and the Qashqai have been forced to stop their traditional migration. As a result, untold damage has been done to their culture. These tribal people are the most colorful and wealthy of all the Persian tribes. The women are dominating and colorful, one of the few women in this part of the world not confined in chadre. They stride about in colorful lurex skirts and jewelry that would make the most outrageous 'hippie' look dull. Their kilims are equally striking and probably the best known of all Persian flatweaves. There is a freedom and boldness in their patterns not found elsewhere.

Qashqai. The weaver of this kilim has taken pleasure in the interplay of shapes and lines, forming a grid of bright colors and areas of contrasting reds, greens, and blues. Circa early 20th Century. 9'4" x 5'4". $5,000.

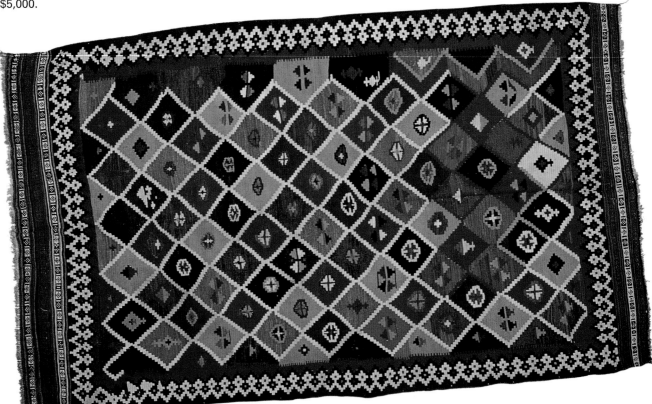

Qashqai This is a beautiful piece, very well drawn, bright and lustrous. It's often hard to differentiate between Lurs and Quashqai; the sheen and quality of the wool are often the only clues. This rug is soft and shiny leading me to categorize it as a fine Qashqai. It also uses cream in the outer borders, which makes it a very beautiful decorative piece. Circa 1940s. 8' x 4'10". $3,500.

Qashqai. This is a dramatic kilim with its bright central diamond motif. The wonderful bright colors of this piece clearly make it a collector's piece. Early 20th Century. 9'2" x 4'8". $4,000.

Above: This diamond pattern is considered very desirable. The rug was constructed using natural dyes and great detail. Every diamond has a different motif. It's a beautifully written rug. The Lurs used all woolen warp and weft threads. 8'3" x 4'11". $5,000.

Below: Another characteristic of the Qashqai rugs are the borders, which are usually finely drawn "laleh" or tulip motif, often linked with a zigzag inner border.

Above: Lurs from southern Iran. This weaver made heavy use of aniline orange and natural dyes for the field. It is a little duller in its color and the overall effect is more subdued than you would imagine. This diamond pattern is considered very desirable. 8'3" x 4'11". $5,000.

Right: Qashqai. This is the most contemporary rug from this region. It's probably from the 1950s-60s. I bought it from a weaver who so intrigued me that just saying no was not an option. Even though it looks a little bright next to all its cousins, it has all the vim and vigor of these colorful people. 8'4" x 5'2". $2,000.

Lurs. This is great example of floating diamond shapes associated with rugs from this area. It's hard to say if it's a Lurs or one of the neighboring tribes, but its slightly duller sheen is enough evidence for me. 1930s-1940s. 7'9" x 4'3". $3,000.

Afshar of Kerman

These rugs from southern Iran are known in the market as Afshars. This area is regarded as the homeland of a large group of Turkic people who are considered unpatriotic to the present Iranian way of life. The province of Kerman is a very isolated area and its textiles are often attributed to Shiraz or Sirjan, bazaar towns for nomadic weavers. Kerman was at one time a rich and prosperous city, most of it being destroyed by earthquakes in the sixteenth century. The present day weavings from the Kerman are heavily influenced by the fine Afshar designs of the nineteenth century, which in turn were influenced by Indian woven and printed textiles. These pieces have an all-over weft-wrapped construction in coarse and loosely spun wool with cotton warps. The field is decorated with two or three central medallions, surrounded by animals and floral motifs. They are very happy rugs, popular with the young and old. Their construction makes them very durable, making both the design and durability great for children's rooms.

Above: Afshar Kerman. This design can be found in Kermans from the 19th Century. 1990s. 9'5" x 3'8". $500.

Right: Afshar Kerman. 1990s. 6'7" x 3'9". $500.

Opposite: Afshar Kerman runners. 1990s. 9'6" x 2'6" and 9'5" x 2'9". $500.

Top: Afshar Kerman 1990s. 6'8" x 3'11". $500.

Center: Afshar Kerman. This one is interesting because of the double row of medallions. 1990s. 6'7" x 3'7". $500.

Bottom: Afshar Kerman. 1990s. 6'8" x 3'11". $500.

Left: Afshar Kerman. 1990s. 6'7" x 3'6". $500.

Below: Note the wonderful abstracted animals on this rug. When I first set up business in America, the San Diego Zoo used to buy these for sale in their gift shop. It's easy to see why.

Afshar Kerman. 1990s. 6'7" x 3'9". $500.

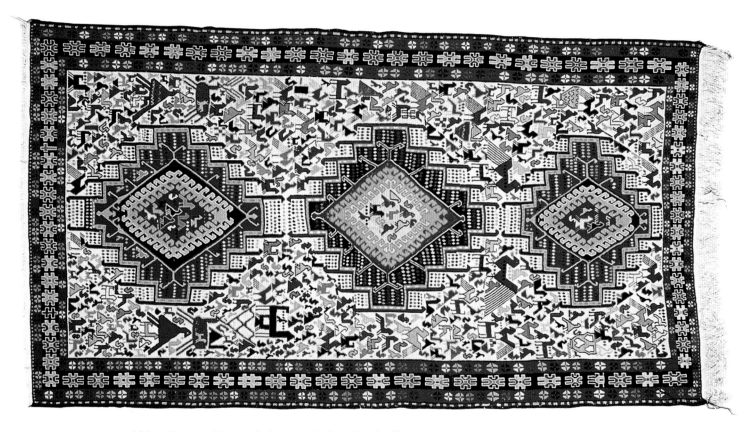

Afshar Kerman. You really have to look at the details of these rugs. This one has a deer with two little babies inside its tummy. 7'3" x 3'9". $500.

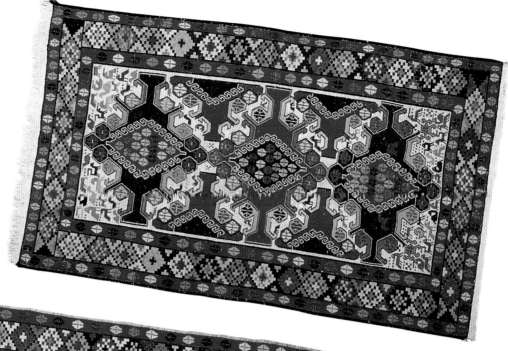

Top: Afshar Kerman. 1990s. 6'5" x 3'8". $500.

Center: Afshar Kerman. 1990s. 6'7" x 4'. $500.

Bottom: Afshar Kerman. 1990s 6'5" x 3'9". $500.

Balouch

In the eleventh and twelfth centuries, these people first arrived in Balouchistan. It was a barren and sparsely populated area, comprised mainly of desert, which lay at the crossroads of Pakistan, Afghanistan, and Iran.

The Balouch weavers used a number of weaving techniques in their kilims. These included weft-faced patterning, where the wool no longer being used is run along the back of the rug. Another is weft wrapping, as found in Soumaks, where a chain stitch effect is created by winding the wool over two warp threads. The third technique, seldom found in kilims, is the knotted pile, where the weft is knotted and cut.

These fine rugs are mainly in darker hues of blues, black, and dark reds with small motifs in cream and ivory wool.

Over the years, any rug that was found in the bazaars of northwestern Iran or Afghanistan were referred to as Balouch, but in fact we can say there are two distinctive groups: Persian Balouch and Afghani Balouch. Within each of these groups are sub-tribes, which I will try and name with each example.

The Balouch have experienced considerable harassment over the last few decades and their rugs are becoming increasingly difficult to find.

Balouch Farah, Iran. Bands of interlocking motifs and patterns. This large rug was made in two pieces; nomadic weavers had to work on looms simple and small enough to be transported. Kilims from the Farah district are always dark in color. These rugs are usually made by the young women of the tribe as dowry pieces. 1960s 9'9" x 6'. $1,500.

Above: Balouch Malaki, Iran. This is a typical example of a Balouch. It was woven in a large rectangular format and two pieces were sewn together with spun goats hair. It is rich and dark in coloration, but with sparkling motifs in ivory wool. 1950s. 9'2" x 5'4". $1,500.

Below: Balouch Malaki, Iran. This rug is tightly woven in a mixture of techniques; weft wrapping and a floating weft give it depth. Its ornate bands of motifs give it great life despite its somber colors. 1950s $1,200.

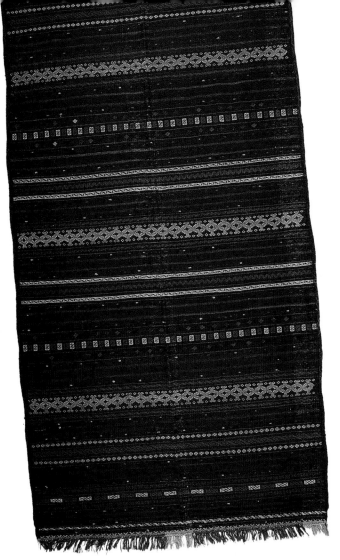

Left: Balouch Maldari, Iran. Simple horizontal bands of plainweave between bands of motifs worked in weft-faced patterning.

Above: Detail of weft face patterning weaving technique.

Below: Qala-i-Nau Hazara Aimaq, Afghanistan. These are a nomadic people living in central Afghanistan. Legend has it they are descendants of Ghengis Khan. The design is one of very ornate bands of pattern with narrow borders on all sides and long end panels in natural brown wool. 1950s. 7'8" x 4'6". $2,000.

Above: Balouch, Afghanistan. This kilim was made near Kandahar in Afghanistan. It could be a "shaffi," which is a cover for bedding and clothes to be stored at the back of the tent, but this has been used as a rug. 1950s. $2,000.

Below: Detail of ivory wool motifs. This symbol represents the tree of life.

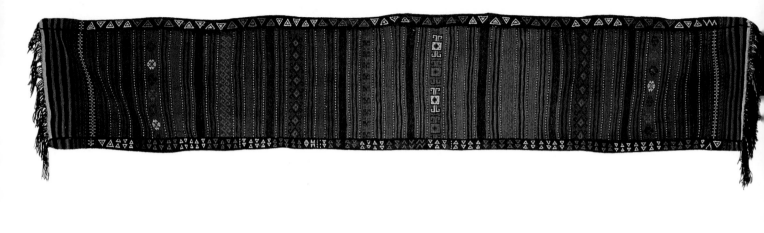

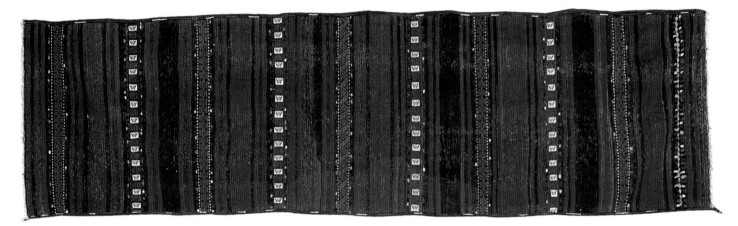

Balouch, Iran. All these pieces have something in common: they are all half rugs. Sometime during the 1980s, local dealers decided they had a better chance of selling these rugs in halves. Often the original piece would be awkwardly matched and quite wide. I have occasionally bought the two pieces and sewn them together again, recreating the original rug. There is nothing wrong with them as rugs, but the price should reflect this fact. These are pieces to bargain for. 1950s. $400.

This next group of rugs is not from the Balouch, but they are usually mistakenly called that. They are Taimani Aimaq. The Taimani are prolific weavers and will copy any rug that is commissioned or hot on the market. They are the weavers who came up with the idea of Afghani war rugs: knotted pieces covered in images of tanks and kalashnikofs. They live in Afghanistan and now many are refugees in Pakistan.

Taimani, Afghanistan. The design of this rug is the Tree of Life. Multiweaving techniques of weft wrapping, knotted pile, and weft-faced patterning. 1990s. 8'8" x 6'2". $850.

Following four pages:
Taimani. These pieces are all eating mats or "soufreh." These are the dining room tables of the nomads. All these pieces are woven in multi-weaving techniques and make great little mats (approximately 4' x 3') for those odd square spots in your house. Old ones are very difficult to find and very expensive; beware — these little pieces are often chemically washed, so what looks old might not be. 1990s $400. aprox size 4 x 3.

Following four rugs: Taimani, Afghanistan. These are the dinning chairs of the nomads. They are long and narrow and always made in bands of weft-faced patterning and knotted pile. These are also used in the tents as filler rugs around larger carpets. They are often used in the West as corridor runners. 1990s $400.

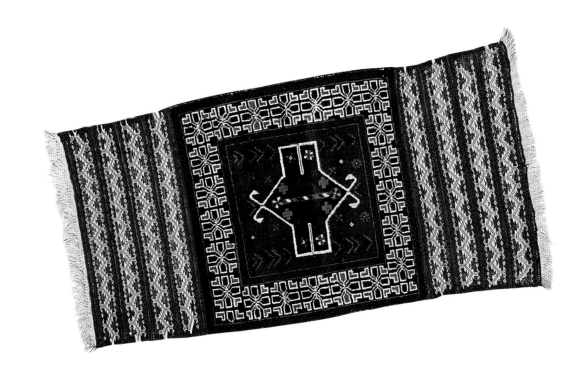

Taimani. Prayer rug in multi-weaving
technique. 1990s. $400.

KILIMS OF THE CAUCUSES

If you were to take a poll amongst dealers and collectors, the weavings from this region would come out on top. The wool from this region is reputed to have inspired Jason to search for the golden fleece.

It's not only the quality of the wool that has fired up collectors, but also the weavers' creativity, their bright clear dyes, and innumerable weaving techniques.

Situated south of Russia with Turkey and Iran on its other borders, this region of mountains and valleys has always been the corridor between the West and the East. Its history is dotted with great and famous voyagers, all of whom left a little bit of their culture and heritage behind. Therefore, it's not surprising that this area is full of many different ethnic groups. There are calculated to be around three hundred to four hundred different tribes and ninety different language and dialects spoken here. You will probably know the area as the newly independent states of the old Soviet Union. I was lucky to be in Northern Pakistan when these areas became independent. Suddenly that tantalizing forbidden land was opened to the world. My first trip there was like being a kid in a candy store, and all subsequent trips have been just as exciting. It's certainly a place for rug collectors to visit, even though exporting your finds are difficult. Visiting museums full of splendid examples makes it well worth the visit.

The Daghestans or Avar

The weavers who come from this area first produced rugs way back in the Middle Ages. We have records of their settlements in the Caucuses from the middle of the sixth century. Most now live to the northeast of this region, close to the Caspian Sea.

Their kilims, now also referred to as Avars, use strong designs and colors, mainly blues and reds. The weavers use powerful abstract motifs, known as rukzals, which have been frequently interpreted as denoting dragons. They also produce designs in softer colors, which often feature the tree of life, birds, and human forms. These abstract textiles work very well in contemporary settings.

The rugs have a distinctive wool texture, and the tight slit-weave technique gives the surface a rigid effect. The fine quality of weaving has meant that these rugs tend to be used as wall hangings and are therefore often found in unusually good condition.

An Avar from Daghestan made of double-lock weave. This is an usual size for a rug from this region. It's a pretty piece, finely made using a double-interlock weave. Circa 1930. 8' x 3'4". $4,000.

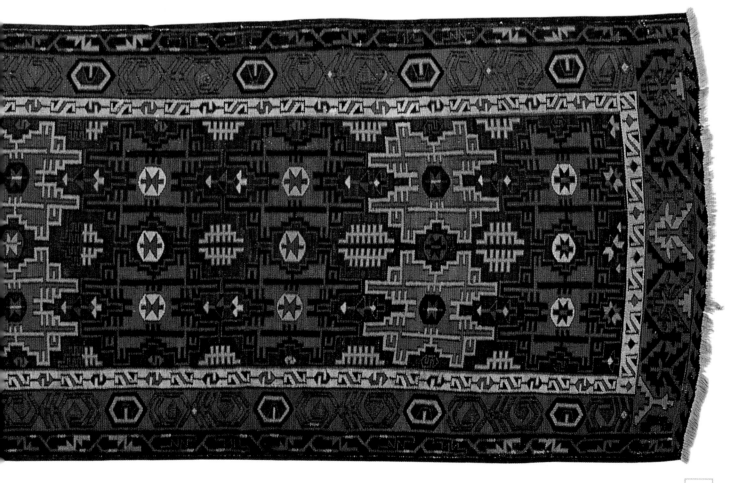

Above: A wonderful kilim from this region, typical in both color and design. The use of yellows and greens make this a strong piece, but its most interesting detail is that the borders are asymmetrical, on purpose. There is no actual explanation for this, except it is a well-known and believed principal that a fine weaver will never make anything perfect, only Allah can do that. The Avar weavers are revered among the Caucus people for their skill. The double-interlock weave of the Avar makes these rugs very durable. All natural dyes with a heavy use of indigo. Early 20th Century. 10'10" x 5'3". Private collection

Below: Detail of border. You can see here the strong use of color and the quality of the weave. There are small details woven in cotton to further heighten the strong contrasts. The motif you see here is considered to represent fighting cocks; a pastime greatly enjoyed by the men of this and other regions in Central Asia.

Above: In this piece you can see trees and human figures all over the central field. The blues and pinks in this piece indicate that it was woven a little later than those with greens and yellows. 20th Century. 14'7" x 4'9". $6,000.

Left: Detail of center motif with human form.

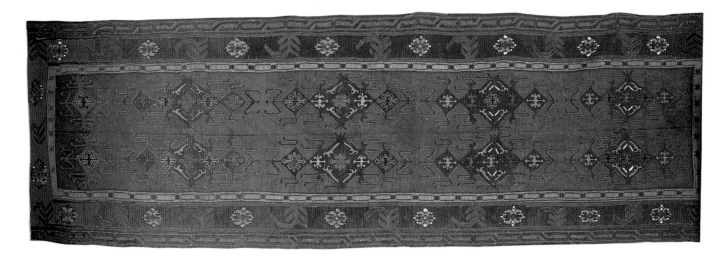

Above: The main field of this kilim is supposed to represent dragons. Woven as a wall hanging, it still has its loops. It's certainly a magnificent piece. It also has the lazy line weaving technique, seen in the large areas of flat blue. Early 20th Century. 15' x 4'6". $7,000.

Below: Detail of the weaving technique known as lazy line, which gives the carpet a ridged effect.

Aove: A great example of the tree of life that the Avar weavers are famous for. Late 19th Century. 14'2" x 3'11". $4,000, because the condition is poor.

Left: A superb example of fine weaving by the Dhagestan weavers. Early 20th Century. 7'4" x 3'4". $4,000.

Soumak

The finest Soumaks are found in Azerbaijan in Central Asia. The name itself comes from the small town of Shemakha, which is just north of Shahsavan. The rugs are unique, with a very particular style of weaving that was first discovered here. Although the technique they invented has subsequently been copied by a number of other tribes, the finest and most refined Soumaks always seem to come from Azerbaijan.

The technique they used is known as weft wrapping. The weaver takes the weft thread and wraps it over two warp threads, bringing it up through the middle, thus creating a style that resembles a chain stitch. This allows for making curves much more easily. The rugs are large and this unique weaving style has proved remarkably durable. It is one of the few flatweaves that come in really large sizes. What's really amazing about these rugs is that they look just like a typical Oriental rug, with none of the tribal naiveté. They use deep red or blue with details in yellow and white and occasionally pink. The designs can be traced back over thousands of years. In fact, elements of their designs can be seen today in knotted pile rugs. It would therefore seem likely that the Soumaks inspired the prolific Persian rug makers of the 19th Century.

This is a particularly sweet rug because of the color changes throughout. Its size is also very attractive.
Early 20th Century. 8' x 4'11". $8,000.

Above: This has all the things that people look for in a classic Soumak. It is large and beautifully designed. These type of pieces remained in great condition, usually because they would only be used for big ceremonial occasions, such as weddings. Their size and magnificence were indications of the bride's wealth. Turn of the century. 12'4" x 8'10". $15,000.

Left: Detail of the arabesque. This symbol appears quite often in these rugs. It's a symbol of infinity and general good fortune.

This is a piece with a wonderful, symmetrical central field. The motifs here strongly resemble crosses, indicating that it could be from Georgia, which is predominately Christian. The colors of this piece are especially good. The fringes are very ornate, almost braided. The rug includes some stylized figures. A nicely written rug, not too busy, the design staying very simple and defined. Natural dyes. Turn of the century. 9'6" x 5'. $10,000.

Soumak from Azerbijan. This is another large formal rug, almost certainly produced for a bridal dowry. The colors are classical rich reds, blues, brown, and ivory. The field is very traditional, with rocket-like motifs bordering three large central guls. Early 20th Century. 12'3" x 8'10". $15,000.

Details of central gul and running dog border. This design can be seen on ancient Greek pottery. You can see here how the weaver has used ivory wool to accentuate the central guls.

Above: Soumak from Azerbijan. This is not a very old piece, though its odd shape makes me think it was made for the local market rather than for export to the West. It's not a piece made with great care or love, but nonetheless it's a handsome rug. Lately many of these have appeared on the market. Their pricing is very different from the older pieces. The sheen and colors of the rug should help you differentiate. 1960-'70. 12'7" x 6'7". $2,000.

Below: This Soumak is from Georgia. It's a totally different motif, coloration, and style, with non-Muslim elements such as crosses. The weavers probably were Muslim, but the predominant population in Georgia is not. A nice piece because the ground is the dye from mulberries, a purplish mushroom color. Early 20th Century. 9'9" x 7'4". $8,000.

Above: Soumak This rug is known as a peacock rug, This particular bird is considered extremely lucky in this part of the world. For the weaver to have used this symbol so often makes me think it was a dowry piece. These rugs are very desirable to a lot of people because they have that comfortable Oriental feel; they are not as tribal or as geometric as many flat weaves. Late 19th Century. 9'6" x 5'3". $10,000.

Left: Close-up of two peacocks. Here you can see two of the abstracted symbols of the peacock. This rug is scattered with such charming representations.

Above: Azerbaijan, Soumak. This rug is really pretty because of the way the weaver used the light-colored wool to detail the guls and the running-dog border. By using such contrasting color on the border, the rug almost seems to float. Early 20th Century. 9'3" x 3'11". $5,000.

Below: Soumak from Georgia. The dimensions of this rug make it more like a wide runner than an area rug. Rugs were popular in these shapes because of the local architecture in Central Asia. Here in the West they work well in a room that has many oriental rugs scattered around the room. 1940s. 10'6" x 5'1". $5,000.

Azerbaijan Soumak. The colors and the details of this rug make it a beautiful piece. It is also an extremely finely woven piece. Its shape falls into the odd category, but what a centerpiece for a collection! Early 20th Century. 10'3" x 5'3". $6,000.

Detail of the border, note the wonderful leaf and flower motifs.

Detail of the central "gul." A '"gul" is believed to be an abstraction of a flower. Here you can see the intricate and fine weaving of this rug.

Above: Azerbaijan Soumak. This rug is special because of its restrained use of color and its fantastic multiple borders. Its central field is the classic diamond medallions, which are very symmetrical. Remember, these weavers did not use a pattern and the more skilled the weaver was, the more symmetrical are the designs. There are four or five different blues in this rug complimented by deep purple and maroon reds. 20th Century. 8'10" x 5'2". $8,000.

Below: Detail of this rug's great borders. Here you can see the four borders. Running dog at the outer edge and a lovely leaf design on the inner one.

Soumak, Azerbaijan. This is a contemporary rug. We took a photograph of the nicest antique Soumak we had and asked the weavers to recreate it. This is an example of a new rug that should be bought. In fifty years it will be worth a lot more money. It was actually made by families that haven't been weaving for fifty or sixty years. We were afraid that the their traditions had been lost, but as you can see from the following details, this was far from the truth. 1998. 9'3" x 6'7". $2,500.

Detail of contemporary Soumak. Note the wonderful fine weaving.

Soumak, Azerbaijan. This is probably the most beautiful Soumak in my collection at the present time. It never fails to bring gasps of delight when shown. The difference between a good rug and a great rug is the "drawing" of it. This is a beautifully drawn rug. Its proportions are perfect. The colors are deep and yet vibrant. and its shape being almost a square is very attractive. A master weaver made this rug. 19th Century. 11'6" x 9'10". $25,000. Private collection.

Detail of a small peripheral "gul."

Detail of a central "gul." Note the fine ivory highlights.

Detail of the borders. The ivory wool is used to define the rug's shape. Note the leaf motifs inside the ivory borders.

These three contemporary Soumak rugs from Northern Pakistan were made in small workshops by very skilled Turkoman refugees using local wool. The major difference is that they are weaving Kasak designs rather than traditional Turkoman designs. The Turkoman weavers are very skilled and can turn their hand to any weaving technique. These rugs will probably never become collector's pieces, but are certainly great handmade rugs at very affordable prices. They are made from hand-spun wool and natural dyes. 5'8" x 6' and 4'10" x 6'10". $1,000-1,200.

New production Soumaks made in Pakistan by Turkoman women. One of the problems with kilim runners is their width. Traditionally such rugs are over 3'6" wide, making them too wide for western hallways. These pieces are narrow and long and have proved to be very popular in the market. Note the great details such as checkerboard edging and braided fringes. They are a great alternative to commercial runners. 12'2" x 3'1". 9'10" x 2'9". 15'6" x 2'11". $1,000.

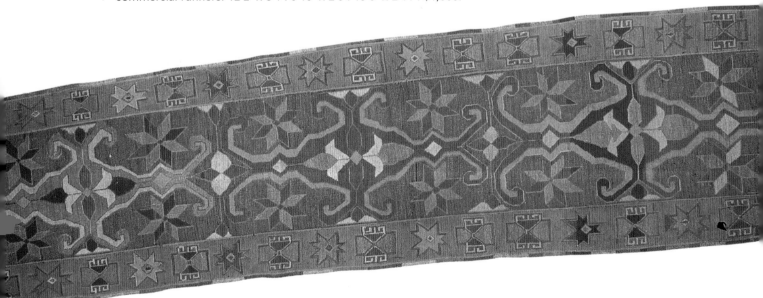

Kuba

These very distinctive kilims take their name from the area known as Kuba in southern Georgia. The rugs are woven with a slit weave and their unique designs aren't found in any other Caucasian kilims. Slitweave is a weaving technique where the weaver changes color by stopping off on a warp thread, changing yarn, and restarting on the adjacent warp thread. Thus a small slit is left between the colors. The designs are often abstract, indented medallions, structured with hooked medallions running down the center of the rug. The borders often show a repeated motif. Kubas are usually highly decorated and the entire rug will be covered with these intricate designs.

Fine rugs are still produced in the area, but the modern rugs are made of coarser wool and use chemical dyes, which means that they lack the beauty and finesse of the earlier pieces.

This piece has all the elements of a classical Kuba kilim. Note the beautifully drawn running border, which resembles a vine. The color of this rug is very sweet and the hand-spun wool extremely fine. A rug like this would be very suitable for a bedroom or a wall hanging. Late 19th Century. 10' x 5'6". $8,000.

This rug has a typical Kuba border, but a very untypical design. Its field is similar to a Shahsavan, but because of its size and very distinctive border, I classify it as a Kuba. The beautiful natural dyes in this rug have faded into soft pastel greens and mustards. Late 19th Century. 10'10" x 5'2". $6,000.

This rug is a great example of the famous Kuba "gul," an inverted medallion that covers the entire field. Its colors are strong and very masculine. 1950s. 10'8" x 6'2". $4,000.

This piece shows how the use of chemical dyes changes the character of rugs. It is still a finely woven rug, but it has become far more bold and bright. 1960s. 11'8" x 6'1". $2,500.

This is another example of a Kuba with large hooked medallions running down the center of the rug. What makes this kilim interesting is its bright, almost contemporary, color pallet and the multiple inverted triangles surrounding the central diamonds. 1950-60. 11'3" x 5'3". $3,500.

There are two major designs in kilims from this area. One is the large, abstracted medallions arranged in an well organized way, and the other is large, central hooked medallions running down the middle of the rug. This a great example of such a rug. The deep blue ground of this piece makes the medallions look as if they are floating. 1940s-50s. 10'4" x 4'11". $3,500-4,000.

Left: Detail of blue background.

Below: Detail of weaver's signature.

Bottom: Detail of fringe showing unbleached warp threads.

Sometimes it's very difficult to be definitive about a grouping of a rug and this is such a case. The coloration of this piece is not typical,but the bold central medallions running down the middle lead me to believe this is a Kuba. This rug is full of images and motifs, another reason to assume it's from Azerbaijan. Post-1950. 11'5" x 7'. $5,000.

We introduced these rugs into the American market in August, 1998. They are produced in Pakistan using hand-spun wool and natural dyes. This piece is a traditional Kuba, the only alteration being its size. 1998. 12'2" x 9'. $3,000.

Contemporary rug woven by Turkoman weavers in Pakistan. The weaving is incredibly fine, using local, hand-spun wool. 1998. 6'7" x 4'10". $850.

Kuba runners designed to fit the typically narrow hallways of western homes. 1998. 9'10" x 2'3". $700.

Cushion covers woven in saddlebag designs from the Caucuses.

Turkoman

No formal borders existed between Iran, Afghanistan, and Turkestan until the late nineteenth century. Turkoman tribes from the Caucuses moved freely in these areas following the traditional paths that their people had used for centuries.

As the political climate changed, many Turkoman adopted a settled lifestyle. A minority continued their old nomadic ways and they continue to make rugs. These are a proud, tough people with a long-standing reputation for fine horsemanship and trading, who fiercely preserve their traditions and skills.

Their kilims, which are large and rectangular, are always woven in one piece. The patterning is often brocaded guls, the Persian word for flower, although over the years this flower has become so stylized that it is no longer figurative. The larger tribes all have their own gul design, which is considered a standard and is a way of easily identifying a particular tribe.

Turkoman rugs are tightly woven and use deep red dye from madder root or pomegranate skins. The guls are often woven in dark browns, blues, and turquoise, with highlights in ivory white wool. Undyed white or brown wool is used for the warps. The weaving technique used is weft-face patterning. The colored wefts are woven to show on the front face of the rug. These rugs were expertly finished and their size and color makes them a versatile addition to almost all interiors.

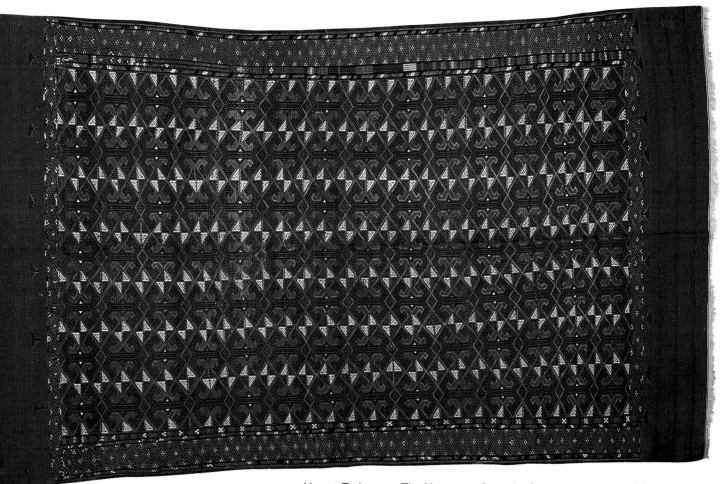

Yomut Turkoman. The Yomut are from the far eastern corner of the Caspian Sea. Their kilims are typically like this one: large rectangles with a madder red ground intricately covered by brocaded guls. This is a fine old piece with an usual checkerboard border. Probably made for a dowry. 9'10" x 5'5". Turn of the century. $10,000. Private collection.

Yomut Turkoman. This is a very unusual rug, I have only ever found two other pieces in this coloration. I can only guess that the weaver was influenced by other rug makers. It also has an unusual field of small motifs in a diagonal pattern. Early 20th Century. 8'4" x 4'9". $6,000. Private collection.

Yomut Turkoman. These rugs are very attractive for western buyers because they have an overall design, They seem very suitable for dinning rooms, as their weaving technique produces robust, hard-wearing rugs that don't become damaged by the constant movement of chairs and feet. 1950s. 6'8" x 12'3". $7,000.

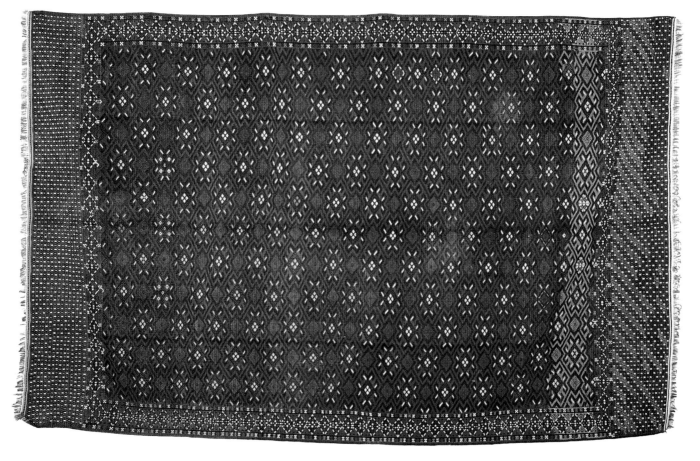

This piece is a rather modern one. Cotton has been used to highlight the guls giving it a nice clean and bright look 1960-'70. 10'7" x 6'6". $2,500-3,000.

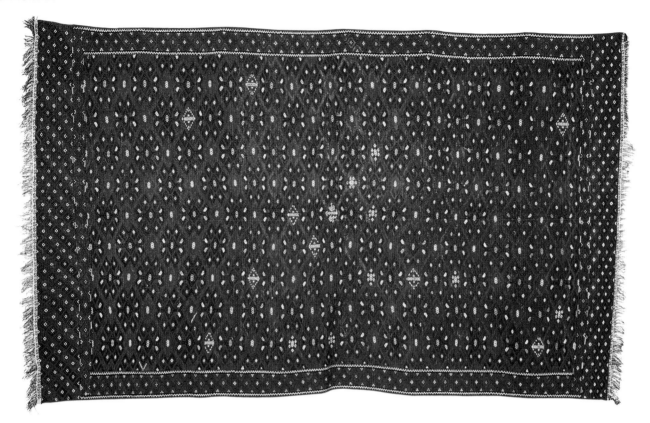

Above: Yomut Turkoman. The weaver here has decided to add a touch of individuality, with a strange checked gul dotted randomly throughout it. It is very appealing, because usually these rugs are very controlled and formal. It could almost be interpreted as the weaver's signature. It also has very nice borders. 1960s. 10'11" x 6'5". $2,500-3,000.

Below: Detail of the maker's mark.

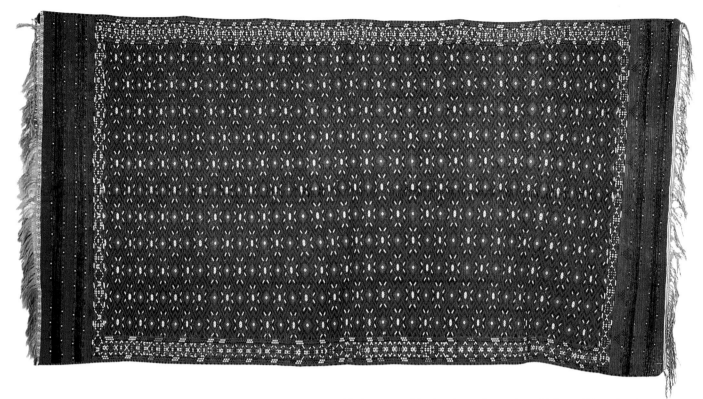

Turkoman with classic end panels, which traditionally do not have brocade work on them, but are simple flat-woven bands of madder red and indigo. 1940s. 11'8" x 6'1". $3,500-4,000.

There's a tremendous use of white cotton in this rug, which is unusual for the Turkoman. It changes the character of the carpet, making it much brighter. One assumes there's been a little influence, probably from a dealer gunning for an export market. Made in Pakistan by Turkoman refugees. When people are displaced, changes are inevitable. 1970-1980. 13' x 7'6. $2,000.

The extensive use of white wool exaggerates the already strong pattern of this rug. Its size and design suggests that this was made as a curtain or door hanging to divide the men from the women in the tents. Mid-20th Century. 7'3" x 3'5". $2,500.

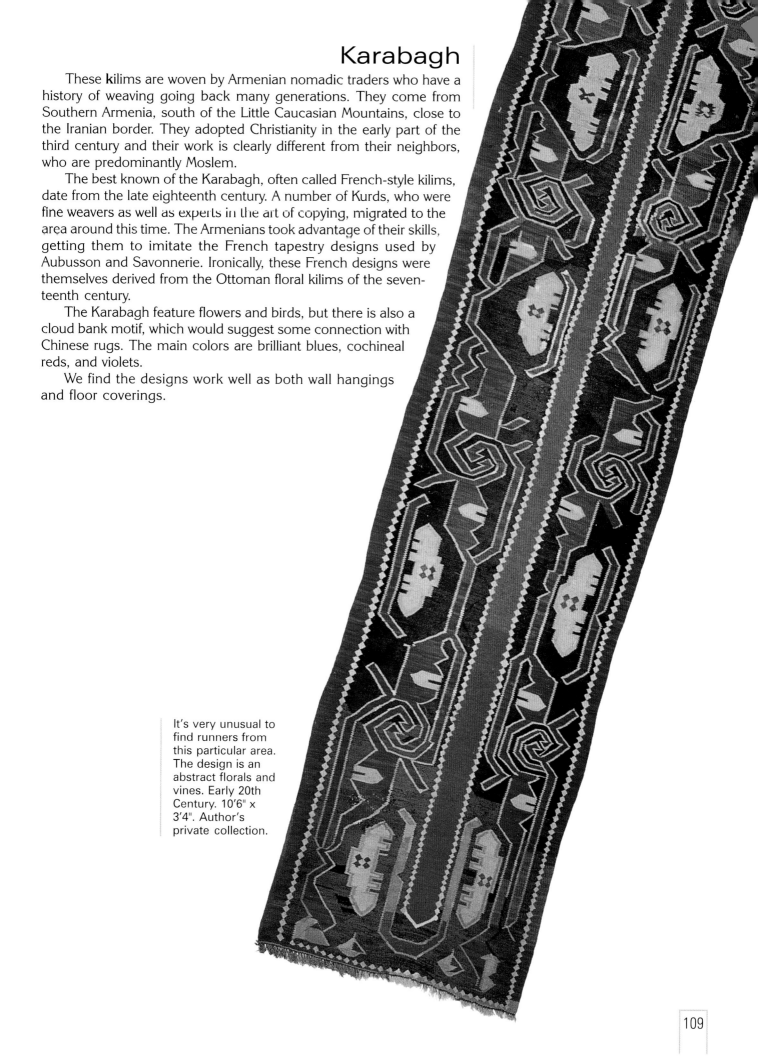

Karabagh

These **ki**lims are woven by Armenian nomadic traders who have a history of weaving going back many generations. They come from Southern Armenia, south of the Little Caucasian Mountains, close to the Iranian border. They adopted Christianity in the early part of the third century and their work is clearly different from their neighbors, who are predominantly Moslem.

The best known of the Karabagh, often called French-style kilims, date from the late eighteenth century. A number of Kurds, who were fine weavers as well as experts in the art of copying, migrated to the area around this time. The Armenians took advantage of their skills, getting them to imitate the French tapestry designs used by Aubusson and Savonnerie. Ironically, these French designs were themselves derived from the Ottoman floral kilims of the seventeenth century.

The Karabagh feature flowers and birds, but there is also a cloud bank motif, which would suggest some connection with Chinese rugs. The main colors are brilliant blues, cochineal reds, and violets.

We find the designs work well as both wall hangings and floor coverings.

It's very unusual to find runners from this particular area. The design is an abstract florals and vines. Early 20th Century. 10'6" x 3'4". Author's private collection.

This rug is a very finely woven decorative piece. Its central field is covered with stylized flowers. Fine hand-spun wool and natural dyes. Early 20th Century. 9'2" x 5'5". $8,000.

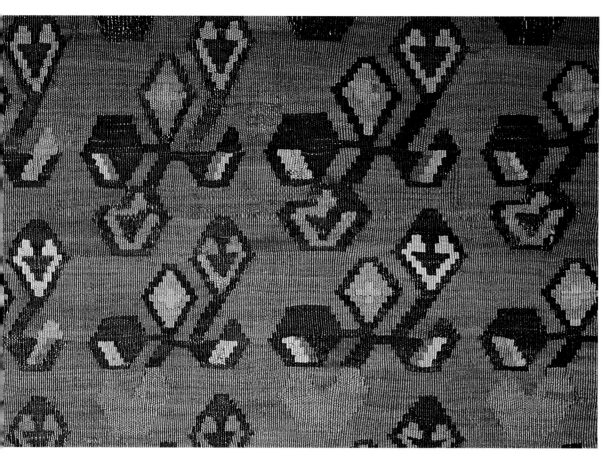

Note how the flower motif has been stylized. Beautiful cochineal dyed background gives this rug its magic.

New production kilim from Pakistan. Hand-spun wool and natural dyes. The design is Karabagh. It's interesting to note that good quality new kilims are often very costly. 1998. 10'5" x 6'6". $2,500.

Shirvan

These are some of the most striking flat-woven rugs, made by the Turkic-speaking nomads who wander over large areas of Azerbaijan and the southern Caucuses.

The weavers use a variety of techniques, from simple slit tapestry weave to complex warp wrapping. Their designs have strongly influenced the Kurds of the Zarand and Bijar, who traveled the same routes.

The Shirvan survive today as a nomadic people, although in recent years a number have settled in the more remote areas of northern Iran. They have stayed true to their traditional styles and weaving techniques, thereby creating both a distinctive kilim and an unequaled quality of work.

They run large, striking motifs across the kilims, separated by narrow bands of a finer pattern. The large motif very often features a star shape, which can range from a simple, eight-pointed triangular design to the more complex crab or spider found in many Turkic rugs.

The rugs are in clear, bright colors. Un-dyed ivory, white, or brown wool are used for the warps and the highly colored designs have narrow borders or none at all.

The finely drawn design and slit weave of this kilim are dramatized by the use of white cotton. The colors are wonderfully clear, as is the tight design. 1940s. 8' x 6'5". $5,000.

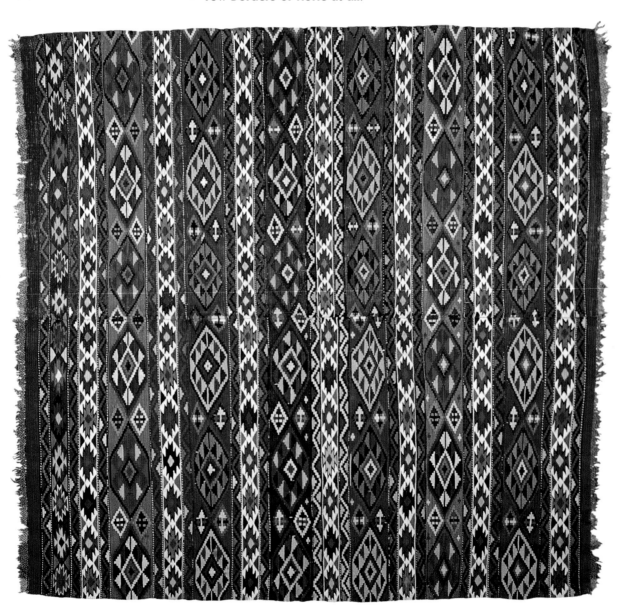

The hexagon motif in this piece can also be fond in other tribal pieces of western Iran. The small filler motifs are what distinguish this as a Shirvan piece. All natural dyes. Late 19th Century. 9'6" x 5'3". $6,000-7,000.

This a typical banded design in a Shirvan kilim. The blues are indigo and the reds cochineal. Note the small geometric pattern running inside the bands of color. Early 20th Century. 9'4" x 4'2". $3,000.

Above: The simplicity of this rug is very appealing in a decorative sense. All natural dyes. Early 20th Century. 10'7" x 5'1". $4,000-5,000.

Right: The weaving technique is what's interesting about this piece; it is far more complex than most Shirvan being a combination of flat weave and tapestry weave. Early 20th Century. 8'9" x 6'9". $5,000.

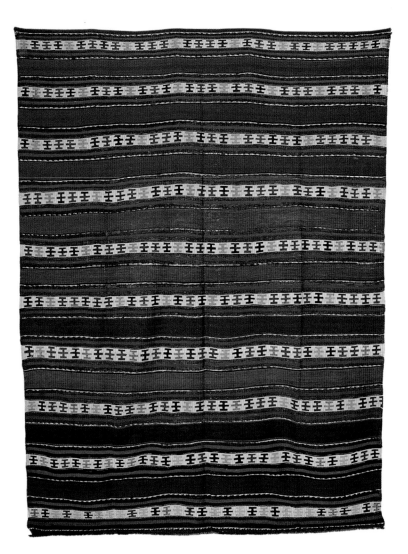

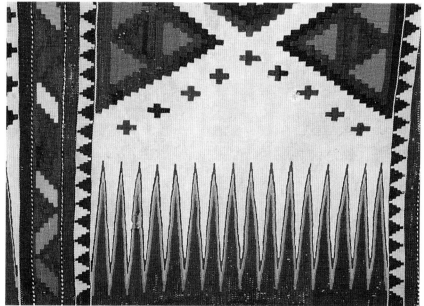

Above: This is half of a large kilim, and such a wonderful piece I couldn't leave it behind. In its entirety, it must have been magnificent. Such a rug would have been made for ceremonial purposes. I hope its demise wasn't due to matrimonial disputes. Early 20th Century. 12'6" x 5'9". $5,000.

Left: Detail of finger border.

Lower left: Detail of a hexagonal motif; a typical Shirvan eight-pointed star.

Shirvan hexagonal motif with crisp bright colors.
Early 20th Century. 11'10" x 6'. $6,000.

Shirvan with an unusual motif: the hexagon has been abstracted. Rather than running off the edge with the gul, which they usually do, they have come up with a completely different shape for the edges. It makes it very interesting and attractive. Early 20th Century. 8'7" x 5'10". $6,000.

This large hexagonal design has been brightened up with white cotton for contrast. This technique is very similar to the Native American Indian eye-dazzler rugs. Early 20th Century. 11'9" x 6'9". $5,000.

There is no real border on these type of kilims, but here the weaver has finished off her bands with the finger motif. 1960s. 10'11" x 6'7". $4,000.

Above: : The weaver of this rug employed tapestry and small bands of warp-weft interface weaving techniques. The all-natural dyes have begun to fade into soft browns and cream. Early 20th Century. 9'8" x 5'5". $3,500.

Below: This is unusual because the central ground is completely covered with guls, rather than the horizontal bands that usually run parallel with the hexagons. It is a busy design, but very attractive. 8'1" x 5'6". Early 20th Century. $2,500.

Above: White cotton has been used in this simple banded kilim. Rather than causing an eye dazzler effect, it heightens the wonderful mustard, reds, and blues in the rest of the design. 8'8" x 5'11". 1920s. $5,000.

Below: This a lovely hexagonal design rug in unusual colors. The principle colors for these rugs are blue and red, but the yellow, greens and black found in this piece are very unusual. 1940-50, dated by the dyes used. 11' x 4'10". $4,000.

SHIRVAN

This is a great example of a Shirvan. It is simple in its design and the coloration is very pleasing. The abundant use of crosses on this piece make it quite unusual. Early 1900s. 4'5" x 8'9". Private collection.

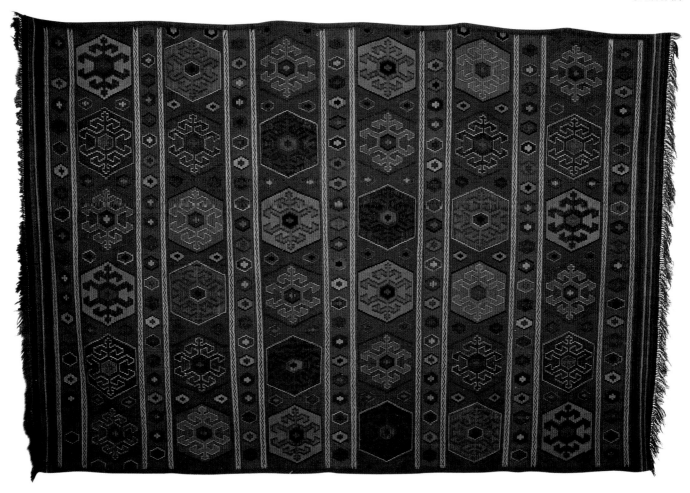

Above: New production kilim made by Tukoman refugees in Pakistan. 1999. 10' x 8' $2,000.

Below: Detail shows the subtle color palette.

SARKOY

These kilims are from an area known as Thrace. Today this area, which is bordered by Macedonia to the west, Bulgaria and the Black Sea to the north, and the Aegean to the south, is geographically part of Turkey. This region, with its dramatic mountains and deep valleys, was inhabited by people of Indo European decent, whose civilization was amongst the earliest in Europe.

Most Thracians are Muslims of Turkish decent, but the area is predominantly inhabited by Greeks and Greek is spoken locally.

Sarkoy kilims are very finely woven in the slit-weave technique and made in one piece. Many feature the tree of life composition, birds regularly appearing either as fillers for the central ground or in the borders.

The shape and size of this rug is quite unique. It's rare to find such pieces unless they were prayer rugs, which this one is not.. Late 19th Century. 4'4" x 3'9". Private collection.

Very finely woven rug. The size makes this one unusual and appealing. Late 19th Century. 5'3" x 3'8". Private collection.

Above: This is a very old piece and a beautiful example of madder red and indigo blue dyes. Rugs of this size were usually made for ceremonial occasions such as weddings and big feasts. Turn of the Century. 10'8" x 11'8". $10,000. Private collection.

Below: Detail of Sarkoy. You can see the expert weaving in this detail. Extra weft threads have been added to make those curvilinear shapes. This is an archaic design that has been used by many tribes.

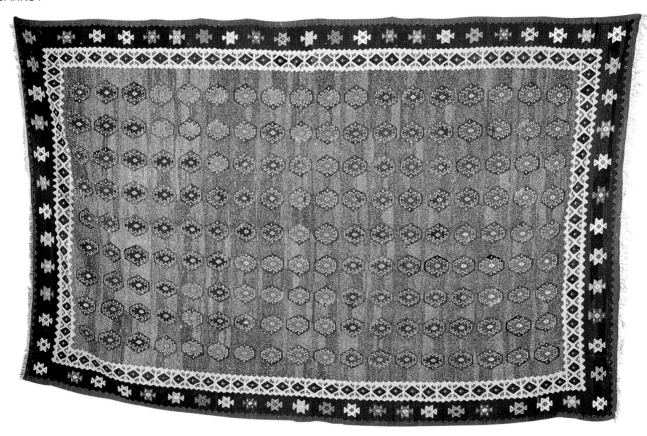

Above: The really interesting thing about this piece is that the central ground is woven with heathered yarn. Heathering is when two different colors of yarn are spun together. It is very unusual in a kilim. 20th Century. 12'2" x 8'. $5,000.

Below: Detail of heathering.

This is a great example of a large Sarkoy. Its motif is the tree of life.
Its dyes are strong and clear, the detail work very precise. A dramatic
rug. Early 20th Century. 11'3" x 10'. $10,000. Private collection.

Detail of vine design and border. Note
the wonderful greens and yellows.

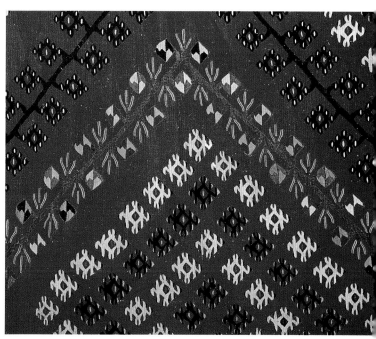

Detail of central motif.
Note the fine detail work.

AFGHANI

Afghanistan is probably the reason I became a rug merchant. It was these people and their way of life that enticed me into this profession. Over the years I have bought and sold thousands of Afghani rugs. I now have three in my collection, and even though they are not particularly the most valuable rugs I own, they are, for me, priceless. My hope is that one day I'll be able to return to Afghanistan, but until then these three pieces are not for sale.

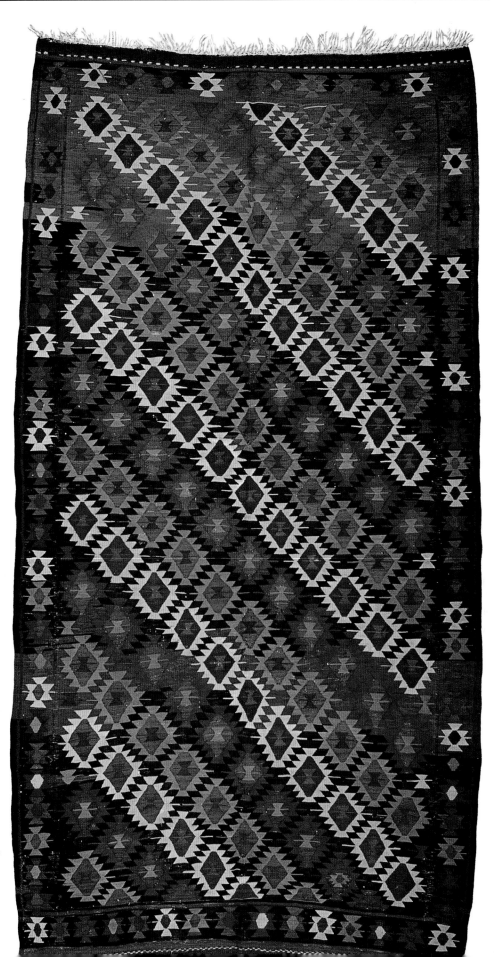

Maimina. 9'6" x 4'11".

Maimina. This is the market town on the Silk Road. It has been a settlement from ancient times and, according to local folklore, was first inhabited by Israelites sent there by Nebuchadnezzer. This dusty town is transformed once you walk into the courtyards of the houses, where a pot of green tea is always produced. This rug is double interlock weave with a combination of greens and yellows.

Maimina. 1960s. 7'10" x 4'10".

GLOSSARY OF TERMS

Aniline: Chemically produced dyes

Abrash: Changes of color within a rug, usually produced by different dye lots

Chadre: Complete covering for women, used whenever outside the family home.

Curved wefts: Extra weft threads are inserted to form curved designs.

Double interlock: A method of weaving where weft threads interlock when new colors are introduced.

Drawing: A term used to describe the design of a rug.

Floating weft: A method of weaving where a simple weave is decorated by using supplementary wefts.

Gul: A term derived from the Persian word flower. It describes the motif found primarily in Turkoman weavings.

Knotted pile: Weaving technique where weft threads are knotted onto each warp thread.

Laleh abrassi: Tulip motif.

Lurex: Brightly colored cloth, usually containing metal threads.

Purdah: A cover or curtain that separates the women's quarters.

Rukzals: Motif used in Dagestan kilims, purported to represent a dragon's mouth.

Safavid: Dynasty in Persian history during the sixteenth and seventeenth centuries.

Slit weave: A method of weaving where the weft threads are tied off and the new color is started on the adjacent warp, thus leaving a slit between blocks of colors.

Warp: The base of the rug. The threads that run from head to toe in any weaving.

Weft: The body of the rug. The yarn that runs from left to right across a weaving, over and under the warp thread.

Weft-faced patterning: A technique where the wefts which create the pattern float on the back of the rug.